WHO IS PLANT KWEEN?

THIS LUSH JOURNEY has been such a lovely adventure, an opportunity for me to dive into the wonders of nature with a sense of eager curiosity—bringing these lil viridescent creatures into the spaces I call home, basking in their intricate glamorous green beauty, and learning the lessons hidden in the folds of their foliage. Through caring for my green gurls, I have learned so much about myself: Who I am as a nurturer; that I need to be better about giving myself the grace, patience, and forgiveness I know I deserve; that healing is like new growth, it's a process that needs time, love, energy, and intentionality; and that at the end of the day I too need sunlight, water, and nutrients to continue to grow into my best self. Now I get to share that journey with you in a holistic way beyond the screens of social media, and I'm excited, gurl!

Being an educator at heart, I started my Instagram account (@plantkween) in 2016 as a way to share the many lessons, lush adventures, and simple joys that comes with being a plant parent. My social media presence has been rooted in a journey of self-care, joy sharing, and community building all through the wonders of these green little creatures we call plants.

YOU
GROW,
GURL!

YOU GROW, GURL!

Plant Kween's Lush Guide to Growing Your Garden

CHRISTOPHER GRIFFIN

HARPER DESIGN

An Imprint of HarperCollinsPublishers

HarperCollins books may be purchased for educational, business, or sales
promotional use. For information, please email the Special Markets Department
at SPsales@harpercollins.com.

First published in 2022 by
Harper Design
An Imprint of HarperCollins*Publishers*
195 Broadway
New York, NY 10007
Tel: (212) 207-7000
Fax: (855) 754-6023
harperdesign@harpercollins.com
www.hc.com

Distributed throughout the world by
HarperCollins*Publishers*
195 Broadway
New York, NY 10007

Cover design by Janay Nachel Frazier
Interior design by Sarah Gifford
Cover and interior photographs by Phoebe Cheong
Endpaper illustrations by shutterstock/Mnsty studioX

ISBN 978-0-06-307704-1
Library of Congress Control Number: 2021038982

PRINTED IN CANADA
First Printing, 2022

For Andrell, my grandmother

My mission in life is not merely to survive, but
to thrive; and to do so with some passion,
some compassion, some humor, and some style.

—MAYA ANGELOU

CONTENTS

INTRODUCTION

The daughter of an avid farmer and gardener, my grandmother was exposed to the wonders of gardening at an early age. She was raised in the small town of Clayton, Georgia, where her mother tended her very own small farm and a beautiful outdoor garden.

HERBS, FRUIT, VEGGIES, my great-grandmother grew them all. My grandmother would often tell me stories about the old farm and how her favorite part of the garden was the little forest of tall sunflowers, her favorite flower.

Like all the Black women in my life, my grandmother was full of magic, soul, light, and life. You'd ride down her street in southwest Philadelphia and easily spot her house because her yard was always lush, green, and in bloom. It was no debate, dahling, her garden was the best garden on the block.

She is, was, and will forever be the original plant queen in my life. When I was about six years old, my grandmother and I would take day trips out to her favorite nurseries in Philadelphia. She would hold my little hand as we stepped inside and wandered around what seemed like a beautiful, endless, lush fairy-tale jungle of a nursery to my young lil aspiring plant kween eyes. I became fascinated by the idea that we could take a small piece of the jungle home with us,

nourish it, and watch it grow. She'd sometimes let me pick out the plants we'd take back with us. She'd welcome them into her plant fam, and whenever I was visiting her green oasis of a home, she'd remind me to water the green gurls I'd picked out . . . she was nurturing the nurturer she saw in me.

Grandmom, you are and forever will be the green goddess who taught me at such a young age that nature can be healing in so many ways. You taught me to honor the green goddess within me and that gardening was a transformative skill that was in our family's blood. When I bought my first plant five years ago, I thought of you. I share my plant parent journey and all that you have taught me in your memory.

For as long as I can remember I've been obsessed with the idea of learning. Yas, dahling, deep down this kween is nerdy, geeky—a student of life, dahling, because there is always something to learn in the big ole classroom called life.

It was during my college experience that I really grew to appreciate my curious mind. As a first-generation college and graduate student, I found that being curious and asking questions was also a tactic for academic survival. I had to proactively seek out resources and ask questions to ensure that I was making the most out of my experience. I also realized that many of my questions were questions other students had, so this kween gave up that fear of being that inquisitive student. If there was something I could not find the answer to on my own, you best believe she was asking all the questions.

And so, dahling, as a lifelong student and educator, I've always had an eager desire to pass on anything that I've found helpful in my own journey. This plant parent journey has taught me so much, and I want to share those lessons, that joy, and that lush botanical love.

I remember when I welcomed my very first green gurl into my home. It was the summer of 2015, and I had just moved into a cute new spot in Bedford-Stuyvesant, Brooklyn, with my two roommates at the time. Gurl, the space was fabulous but lifeless, banal, and cold. If you know this kween well, you'd know that she is all about warmth, bright colors, and LIFE! So I figured this would be the perfect opportunity to pay homage to

the memory of my green goddess of a grandmother and search for my very first plant.

It was a warm Saturday afternoon and I pranced on over to a local hardware store, and the search began! Looking through the lush foliage, I came upon a Marble Queen pothos. The uniqueness of how her iridescent green-and-white leafy vines were growing out of her nursery pot caught my eye immediately. As I took a closer look and began to inspect her foliage, I realized that she was a green gurl that needed a bunch of TLC. Some of her leaves had begun to brown and yellow, other leaves were drooping downward as if she needed a drink of water to perk her up. Gurl, I was nervous! I had always had a slight fear and anxiety that I would be unable to keep plants alive, growing, and thriving. Would I have a green thumb like my grandmother? Would I be able to honor her memory one day with a lush garden of houseplants?

I looked at that struggling Marble Queen pothos, and at that moment I made a deal with myself:

1   I would strut into this plant parenthood journey leading with a sense of curiosity, fun, and joy.
2   I would put that beginner plant parent anxiety and the myth of having a green thumb to the side.

"Through caring for plants, I have learned how to better care for myself. I am better at giving myself grace, patience, and forgiveness."

3   I would explore, build, and connect with the community of plant people who love nature just as much as I do.

Dahling, I welcomed that Marble Queen pothos into my home that day and so began my very first step into the botanical wonders of plant parenthood. I repotted her into a cute terra-cotta planter, pruned some of her leaves, soaked her soil with a fresh drink of water, placed her in a bright, sunny spot, and I left her alone to let her get adjusted to her new home. Hunty, when I tell you she grew! Within a couple of weeks she was growing with a lush fierceness! With some tender loving care and patience (you can't forget patience, gurl), this plant rewarded this nurturer with the simple joy of growth. There was no turning back at that point; I was a devoted plant parent from that moment on.

I started investigating other plant shops in Brooklyn, taking weekend plant-shopping-adventure bike rides to the various shops that popped up on Google Maps. I leaped into researching how to take care of my growing plant family, and eventually started documenting and sharing my botanical fascination and plant parent journey via Instagram.

Through caring for plants, I have learned how to better care for myself. I am better at giving myself grace, patience, and forgiveness. I now understand that the healing and growth of my own heart, mind, body, and soul takes time, love, energy, and intentionality. Putting that love, care, and attention into my plants has honestly provided me with practice and enabled me to put that same amount of love, care, and attention into my own Black queer femme being. The journey of self-care, self-love, and self-fulfillment via plant-care.

And so, five years later, this plant kween has over 200 green gurls in her lil Brooklyn apartment, has gone on numerous botanical adventures, has learned a ton about houseplant care and self-care, and has connected and built friendships with amazing plant people. I'm just overjoyed that I get to share all of this with each and every one of you. This book is filled with that Black queer nonbinary femme plant parent joy! This book is a fun collection of tips, tools, and experiences (and fabulous photos) that have been helpful for me in caring for my green gurls and caring for myself. Plant-care is self-care, dahling. So, I thought I'd share some of my journey with you. Get ready for all the viridescent vibes, hunty!

Let's get lush!

PART 1

BECOMING A PLANT PARENT HOW TO GREEN UP YOUR SPACE

CHAPTER 1

FINDING YOUR GREEN THUMB

Anyone and everyone can have a green thumb, dahling! The only regret I've ever had throughout this entire plant parent journey was not starting this botanical adventure sooner! Pre-plant parenthood, I was anxious about my ability to care for houseplants. I had a fear that I would not be able to keep these living, breathing creatures alive, keep them growing, keep them thriving. I had a fear that maybe I was a kween who just lacked a green thumb. Eventually, I had to put that fear and anxiety to the side and take a leap of faith into the lush green foliage that is being a plant parent, strutting into this adventure with a sense of curiosity, fun, and joy!

AS AN EDUCATOR, I am always fascinated by the history of common phrases, their origins, and how they came to be, because language—the words we use—is important! Whether you have plants or not, you've probably heard the expression "having a green thumb." This notion of inherently having or not having "an exceptional aptitude for gardening or for growing plants successfully" (thanks, Dictionary.com) is simply anxiety provoking, and frankly, this kween just ain't got time for that kind of lingering pressure. So I did some research on when, where, and why this phrase came to be. According to *The Old Farmer's Almanac*, it has two possible origins: It is said that King Edward I developed a love of green peas and kept a dozen of his servant gardeners shelling them. Apparently, the most proficient sheller, judged by the green stains on his fingers, was richly rewarded. You'll notice that this story is not only silly but doesn't really have anything to do with gardening. More plausible is the observation that repeatedly handling clay pots encrusted with algae often rubs off and stains a gardener's thumb (and probably fingers) green.

• • •

AFTER DOING THIS lil word-history research, I knew that it was time for me to redefine what having a green thumb meant for my own botanical journey, just as it had been redefined throughout history. I remember when I asked my mom her thoughts on the common idea that one must have a green thumb in order to take care of plants. She replied, "Oh, what is a green thumb, really? You just need to know what plant fits well with you—a little research, patience, and a whole lotta love is all you need when it comes to gardening."

She looked over at my dad, motioning for him to give his thoughts. He said, "Couldn't have said it better, dear. Never thought I was good at gardening, but your grandmother and your mother showed me that anyone can do it and do it well if they put their minds and hearts into it."

My parents said it best. Nothing about having a green thumb involves inherent talent or a divine gift for gardening—it's something you build and grow into over time through patience, intentionality, dedication, the experience of trial and error, and a lot of plant parent fails and successes.

I remember when I was a plant parent newbie just beginning to build my plant fam, I would go plant shopping and pick up any green gurl that caught my eye. This resulted in a kween purchasing plants that were either too difficult for me to take care of at the time or simply weren't a match for this beginner plant parent. But she's come a long way since then, hunty!

I've learned to let my curiosity and passion for learning lead me in this journey, and this mindset has certainly helped me through my plant fails. Cuz, hunty, losing a green gurl is hard for any plant parent! While this kween has over 200 healthy green gurls in her apartment, it took five years to grow a plant fam that fits my lifestyle, my habits, and my space. I've learned so much in these last five years that I generally know which plants don't do well in my home, which ones do well, and which ones just thrive with me. It's been a process I have learned over time. There may be green gurls that are not a match for me at this point, and, gurl, that's okay! I also know that I have tons more to learn because you can never stop learning, dahling.

THIS KWEEN OCCASIONALLY buys two of the same plant and will place them in different parts of her apartment just to see how they fare in slightly different conditions. While I'm a huge fan of googling plant care tips and seeking advice from my amazing community of plant friends, I also find that a lil planty experimentation can be fun and exciting. And while Google can be an accessible best friend when it comes to plant care research, sometimes the tons of information I pull up is contradictory. I've come to use plant care tips as a general guideline because no one knows my microclimate (my apartment) better than I do. Plant parenthood is quite a journey, dahling, and I intend to continue to have fun with it all!

As you ease yourself into the lush adventures of plant parenthood, here are five thangs to keep in mind that I've found to be helpful during this botanical journey.

1
PATIENCE AND PREPARATION ARE KEY, DAHLING!

As much as you may want to skip on over to your local nursery or plant shop, load up your cart with a bunch of greenery, and instantly fill your space with green gurls galore, it's important to take your time with this journey and not rush into it. Be patient with yourself and enjoy the process as you do your research on the best plants for you and your lifestyle. Are you a kween on the go, traveling often? Some plants are extremely resilient and hearty and actually thrive with a little neglect here and there. Do you have pets or small children? Some plants are extremity toxic if ingested, so nontoxic/pet-friendly/kid-friendly green gurls would be the way to go. Do you get that icky feeling when it comes to insects? Some plants are less prone to those creepy-crawly pests. These are the kinds of questions you should be asking and exploring about yourself before you embark on this journey.

2
GIVE YOURSELF GRACE, KWEEN!

Brace yourself for this one, gurl: Sometimes plants die. It happens. We all have that plant or plants that are supposed to be "easy" to care for but as soon as we bring that kween into our homes, she struggles. Even though we've done our research, it happens. It's the territory that comes with being a plant parent. Perhaps that green gurl and you are not a match right now, and that is okay! I haven't kept count of the plants I've sent to the lil botanical garden in the sky, cuz she ain't about that life, dahling, but I have always used these unfortunate experiences as opportunities to learn, grow, and do better next time. Each time a plant leaves me, I make note of what could have gone wrong. I inspect what's left of the leaves, I take a look at the roots, I note where the plant was placed in my apartment, and then I usually take the remains to my community compost bin. So, for all the new plant parent kweens out there, do not be devastated if you kill one, two, or even a few plants—it happens. Learn from your mistakes, move on, and do better the next time around! Forgive yourself, gurl, and go plant shopping!

3
BE CURIOUS, GURL.

Let your passion for greenery lead you in this adventure! The more you let yourself wander into the vast world of horticulture and wonders of indoor gardening, the better informed you'll be when it comes to caring for your green gurls. Whether it's reading articles online, picking up a gardening book, or chatting with your plant friends or the amazing plant people who work at your local plant shop, allow yourself to get lost in the greenery of it all. Even with common plant parent struggles, I look at each and every one as an opportunity to do better for my green gurls, an opportunity to be creative in remedying that struggle, and a moment to potentially learn something new. So, get like Curious George, gurl, and let curiosity and a passion for learning lead you in this adventure!

4
BE OPEN TO LEARNING THE LESSONS YOUR PLANT FAM CAN TEACH YOU.

There is a simple and intricate beauty that comes with nurturing nature and watching her grow. This love for these green little creatures we call plants has opened pathways for me to deepen and explore my own methods and strategies for self-care. Through caring for them, I have learned how to better care for myself. I am better at giving myself grace, patience, and forgiveness, understanding that the healing and growth of my own heart, mind, body, and soul takes time, love, energy, and intentionality. Putting that love, care, and attention into my plants has honestly provided me with practice and enabled me to put that same amount of love, care, and attention into my own Black queer non-binary femme being—the journey of self-care, self-love, self-fulfillment via plant-care, dahling. So let your green gurls teach you their ways, because we can learn a lot from these kweens.

5
HAVE FUN!

It is my hope that at the end of the day plants bring you joy, that you get to bask in that happiness, and that this adventure is a fun and wild one (pun intended, dahling!). Have fun with the beautiful process of plant parenthood and treat yourself to some greenery. You deserve it, gurl!

QUICK NOTES

How to convince yourself, partner, family member, roommate, or any other loved one why you need more green gurls in your life:

→ House plants improve the air quality in our homes. House plants are nature's indoor air purifiers, taking in the carbon dioxide we breathe out and producing oxygen. During photosynthesis, plants absorb carbon dioxide and release oxygen. Many house plants also remove toxins from the air, increase humidity (as part of their photosynthetic and respiratory processes, plants release moisture vapor), and reduce airborne dust levels. All these things are great for our bodies!

→ House plants reduce stress and can positively impact one's mental health, mood, and overall well-being and creativity! In moments when I am feeling stressed or anxious, I tend to turn to my green gurls. Whether I'm pruning them, dusting off their leaves, watering them, or checking for any new leafy growth, they allow me a space to quiet my mind and calm my anxiety.

→ House plants can have a positive impact on your productivity, as compared to being in spaces without them! My werk space is filled with greenery, and when a call ends early and I have an extra five minutes until my next call, I'll tend to my green gurls, refill the humidifier, or check to see if they need a drink of water. Sometimes I'll just pick one plant and I'll check to see if there is any new growth or maybe I'll notice a fine detail that I hadn't before. Sometimes I'll just look upon my green gurls, I'll take a couple of intentional breaths in and out . . . and they've done it, my green gurls have reset me. Five minutes later I'm ready for my next meeting, replenished and ready to get to werk!

CHAPTER 2

CHOOSING THE RIGHT PLACE AND ASSESSING YOUR SPACE

Alright, dahling, we already know that the lush wonders and adventures of plant parenthood are irresistibly fabulous, so let's dive into the very first step of greening up your life: assessing your space! The three main factors you want to consider are:

1 Sunlight
2 Humidity
3 Temperature

BEFORE GREENING UP ANY SPACE and breathing life into it, it's always important to see what you are werking with in your microclimate! So, take your time, be patient with yourself, and enjoy the process of learning more about the space you are in, cuz it's gonna be a wild ride!

SUNLIGHT

HAVE YOU EVER SAT in your apartment, house, or office and watched the sunlight dance across the walls? It's a beautiful thing to witness and it's typically the first thing I do when I'm thinking about adding plants to any space, because light is a fundamental essential when it comes to any green gurl growing and thriving. Just as sunshine is important and tells our bodies when we should be sleeping and when we should be awake, the same is true for our green gurls! While light and dark tells our bodies when to produce the hormone melatonin, which cues tha bawdy to feel sleepy, light and dark tell our green gurls when to produce the hormone auxin, which controls their growth and development.

I'm sure you've seen those cute time-lapses of plants dancing in the sunlight; well, gurl, those green gurls are moving in small ways to maximize their exposure to that energy-giving sunlight. During the day they are soaking up the sun, converting the light into sugar, and creating the energy they need to survive (photosynthesis).

I tend to put my green gurls into three lighting categories:

1   Bright, with some direct light (cacti and succulents)
2   Bright, indirect light (*Monstera, Ficus elastica, Alocasia*)
3   Low-light tolerant (snake plant, pothos, ZZ plant)

So, let's get into the details with three easy steps to help you get a better sense of the sunshine that your space is serving.

SOUTH-FACING ⓘ @plantkween

→ And just for clarification, dahling: Direct light is pretty much what it sounds like, meaning that green gurl receives direct, unobstructed sunlight. Indirect light is when that green gurl is in a light-filled environment but the sun's rays are not directly hitting her leaves.

WHIP OUT THAT COMPASS!

Whenever I enter a new space, I am always curious about how much sunlight it gets throughout the day and I tend to use the compass app on my phone. The directions the windows face allow me to gauge the amount of light shining through.

SOUTH-FACING WINDOWS

These windows are highly sought after by plant parents, for in the Northern Hemisphere the sun follows a slightly southern east-to-west arc across the sky, flooding these windows with bright light throughout the day. In general, these are perfect windows for a space in which to build a plant family because you have the flexibility to be creative and intentional about where you place your green gurls based on the amount of light they enjoy. With these windows, remember to be careful about plant placement, as too intense sun can give the plants sunburn, gurl! I tend to keep my cacti and succulents right on the sills of these windows, since they enjoy bright light with some direct sun. As for my green gurls who prefer bright, indirect light, I place them at least 2 feet from a south-facing window or cover my window with a sheer curtain to filter the light.

NORTH-FACING 📷 @welcometothejjunglehome

NORTH-FACING WINDOWS

These windows create low-light conditions, not allowing much direct sunlight, and make your space on the shadier side with even, ambient light throughout the day. This is perfect for cultivating tropical rainforest understory plants that thrive in shadier lighting conditions. I suggest those green gurls that can tolerate lower lighting for spaces with these windows, such as the snake plant, the pothos, the ZZ plant, the Chinese evergreen, or the *Dieffenbachia*, just to name a few.

EAST-FACING WINDOWS

East windows tend to be brightest in the morning, benefiting from that sunshine when the rays are not quite as strong. Green gurls that prefer moderate sunlight (low to ambient/indirect light) typically do well in spaces with these windows. The umbrella tree, Calathea, the prayer plant, and the purple shamrock are just a few green gurls that can thrive in these lighting conditions.

WEST-FACING WINDOWS

West windows tend to get a long period of direct light, with full afternoon and evening sun, usually missing the hottest, most intense part of the day. Although they don't get the same intensity of light as south-facing windows, west-facing windows are a good place for your sun-loving green gurls.

WEST-FACING @apartmentbotanist

AND SINCE WE ARE on the topic of light, dahling, I thought I'd provide some helpful notes about utilizing artificial grow lights to help your green gurls if your lighting situation is not ideal:

→ Violet-blue light in the 400- to 520-nanometer range encourages chlorophyll absorption, photo-synthesis, and that good green gurl growth, hunty.

→ LED grow lights are my fav simply because they are energy-efficient, they have an ultra-low heat output, and they offer an ideal light spectrum range that my green gurls enjoy.

→ Hanging or placing grow lights 6 to 8 inches over your green gurls is the best arrangement, as it mimics natural sunlight from overhead and exposes all sides and leaves of that green gurl to the artificial light. Be sure to read the instructions on the grow lights you purchase to confirm the optimal distance.

Darkness is actually very important for your green gurls' growth cycle. During the day, sunlight helps these kweens produce energy through photosynthesis. At night, however, your green gurls break this energy down for growth and flowering in a process called respiration. Plan on giving your kweens at least eight hours of darkness per day . . . so use those grow lights in moderation, hunty.

EAST-FACING   @welcometothejunglehome

SUNSHINE, SHADOWS, AND SHADE . . . OH MY!

As the sun dances across the sky, it moves across your space. That sunshine will hit at different angles, cast chic shadows, be dimmed by obstructions outside your window, and take various shapes and shades throughout the day. So sit, take note, and watch the sun as the rays dance across your walls. There may be a certain wall that gets a ray of bright light in the afternoon, but it fades as the evening approaches. There may be a corner that gets consistent bright, indirect light throughout the entire day, which only fades once the sun has set. There may be a nook that is dimly lit, or gets no natural light during any part of the day.

Now when it comes to measuring the light that enters your space, I have a fabulous lil activity you can dive right into.

THE SHADOW TEST
Pick a part of the day when the sunlight seems its brightest in your space; typically the middle of the day—between 10am and 4pm—is the best time frame. After observing how the sun moves through your space, go stand in the spot you want your green gurl to live.

Use your hand, foot, or an object (like this book!) to cast a shadow. If the shadow is:

→ strong and clearly defined = bright, with some direct light

→ a bit fuzzy but you can still make out the silhouette = bright, indirect light

→ faint and lacks much definition = low light

→ nonexistent = no natural light

The intensity of the light inside the space you hope to green up may change and vary based on the season. There may be spots in your space that get bright light during the summer months and lower light in the winter months. Repeat this lil activity during different times of the year and adjust your green gurls as needed. Gurl, my previous apartment didn't have the best light, so I had some of my plants on a mobile utility cart and rolled them to wherever the sun was shining that season—she had to get creative!

STEP 3
MARK THAT SPOT, DAHLING!

Now that you've had a chance to get a sense of the overall amount of sunlight in your space and have narrowed it down to a specific spot where it hits just right, mark that spot with some tape. Take a step back and check the spot out as it relates to the rest of your space. Is this a spot for a small, medium, or large plant? Does the place fit the foot traffic of your space? If the tape is on a spot on your wall, would a shelf or a ceiling hanger work for that space? If the tape is on a spot on your floor, would you want to place your plant directly on the floor or prop it up with a plant stand? Let your creativity wander.

HUMIDITY

HAVE YOU EVER STRUTTED into a lush greenhouse at a botanical garden and been hit with a wave of moisture in the air? Your glasses fog up and your skin begins to serve that dewy realness?! Well, hunty, that is humidity and it is often a forgotten key ingredient when it comes to caring for our green gurls and creating an indoor environment that allows them to thrive. Many of these kweens come from tropical and subtropical regions where they flourish in the loamy, humid underbrush of larger forests and jungles. Our indoor spaces are quite different from these lush lands, and as a plant parent, my ultimate goal is to try my best to replicate and mimic the natural environment that my kweens hail from. After all, dahling, I want them to feel right at home!

Most green gurls need some level of humid air in order to serve that green lusciousness. The pores through which these kweens breathe lose most of their moisture when the air surrounding them is dry, and they can't always replace that loss through the water their roots absorb. Thinner leaves mean a greater need for humidity. Thick, leathery, or waxy leaves, or those covered with hair, can usually werk through that dry air and tend to have other adaptations for water retention. Signs that the air could be a bit dry include curled leaves and dry and crispy leaf tips, as well as a frequent need for watering.

Here are some key thangs that have been helpful for me as I've werked to maintain a level of humidity in my space that my green gurls enjoy.

MEASURING HUMIDITY

Get yourself a hygrometer, gurl! This cute gadget is one of the best ways to measure the humidity level in the space you are looking to green up! Its basic function is measuring the moisture in the air, and I've

found it available at local nurseries, hardware stores, and online. Hygrometers measure both humidity and temperature. In my current apartment, I have three digital hygrometers, which are fabulous because they are tiny and portable, and I have them placed throughout my space to get a better sense of the humidity levels in my lil indoor Brooklyn oasis.

Go to the spot in your space that you are hoping to green up, place the hygrometer there, and see what percentage of humidity that particular spot is serving.

→ 60 to 90 percent: Gurl, if the gadget is reading in this range, then make sure you open up a window to allow for airflow. Too much humidity indoors can be harmful for our bawdy and for our home, causing mold, musty odors, rot, and structural damage, and we ain't got time for that. For context, dahling, the average humidity for the Amazon rainforest during wet season is 88 percent!

→ 40 to 60 percent: Most homes are typically in this range, and a majority of green gurls thrive in these humidity conditions. I tend to keep my home humidity between 50 and 55 percent, and my green gurls seem to be enjoying it cuz they are serving that viridescent vibe, dahling. Airflow throughout the space is still crucial at these levels, so I open a window or turn on a fan when the levels reach near 60 percent.

> 10 to 40 percent. Below 40 percent means this kween is waking up with that raspy dry cough in the morning, and she is not about that life. These levels tend to be caused by the drying effect of central and artificial heating. While my cacti and succulent kweens are fine in these conditions, a majority of my green gurls tend to experience curled leaves and dry and crispy leaf tips at these levels.

WAYS TO ADD HUMIDITY

I've always struggled with maintaining my ideal (50 to 55 percent) humidity levels in my space. Living in Brooklyn, a kween has to be intentional and strategic with her green gurls when faced with that sizzling hot heat + air conditioners during the summer months and that frigid, crisp cold + heaters during the winter months. These harsh seasons impact the levels of humidity in my space, but, dahling, she has done her homework and is happy to report that maintaining my ideal 50 to 55 percent has gotten easier over time. Below are three effortlessly easy ways I've increased the humidity in my space.

1.
GROUP YOUR
GREEN GURLS!

As a part of their photosynthetic and respiratory process, plants breathe moisture into the air through a process called transpiration. Our green gurls release roughly 97 percent of the water they take in through their roots, which makes perfect sense because after I water the kweens in my lil plant nook the humidity level in the room always increases.

So by bringing those kweens together you are increasing the humidity of the air around them.

2.
INVEST IN A HUMIDIFIER, HUNTY!

I bought my first humidifier as I entered my second year of plant parenthood, after having realized the tragic reality that the dry air in my apartment was causing my green gurls' leaves to brown, shrivel, and eventually fall to the floor like autumn leaves. I stick with evaporative and cool-mist humidifiers, as these machines do not generate heat that can harm my green gurls if the unit is placed too close. The size of the humidifier depends on the space you are werking with. The larger the space, the larger the humidifier; the smaller the space, the smaller the humidifier. I tend to run only my medium-size cool-mist humidifier if the hygrometer reads below 40 percent, and I let

the full tank run out of water (takes about an hour). If the humidity gets above 60 percent, she's opening a window or turning on a fan to get some air circulation + flow going.

3.
GIVE YOUR GREEN LITTLE KWEENS A SHOWER!

Most of my high-humidity kweens are right at home in my bathroom, the most consistently humid spot in my apartment after I take myself a cute warm shower. Some of my other tropical kweens that enjoy humidity but can't fit into my bedroom I usually bring into the shower when watering them and let cool/room-temp water lightly sprinkle them. My staghorn fern (Ms. *Platycerium superbum*) that is mounted on wood in

my bedroom is a plant that I often take off the wall and place in the shower for a few minutes. This routine is particularly helpful in keeping her thriving, as it mimics the downpour of rain she is used to in her natural habitat.

Caring about and being aware of the humidity levels in my apartment has been so helpful for my green gurls and my own bawdy. Simply put, by keeping a healthy humidity level in my space I'm helping my plants retain more moisture and ensuring optimal transpiration, which is key for that new growth. And I'm creating great conditions for my own bawdy to experience less dust, dander, symptoms from allergies, that raspy dry cough, and all the other tragic thangs that come with dry air.

TEMPERATURE

GRAB THAT HYGROMETER, gurl, cuz you ain't done with it yet! It's time to take your microclimate's temperature! With a majority of our green gurls being native to tropical and subtropical regions, these kweens thrive in temperatures that are very much like those in our homes. The optimal scene for most of our green gurls ranges anywhere from 65° to 75°F (18° to 24°C)! And while a majority of these kweens can tolerate temperatures slightly above and below what they prefer, here are some thangs to be mindful of as you temperately set the mood.

WHEN THANGS GET TOO HOT

Whether you're living in a climate that is seasonally warm or you live in a city like Brooklyn that serves the occasional heat wave realness, it's important to not let the temperature in your green lil indoor oasis get too hot. I've found that temperatures above 75°F (24°C) cause some of my green gurls to go into distress. Soil drying out too quickly, leaves wilting, becoming crispy with dry edges and eventually falling off, are just a few of the signs that your green gurls need to escape that trapped heat and cool down.

WHEN THANGS GET TOO COLD

Just like Goldilocks, our green gurls don't like it too cold either! Most green gurls native to the tropics begin to struggle at temperatures below 50°F (10°C) and may take a permanent trip to the botanical garden in the sky at temperatures at or below 40°F (4.4°C). And while plants may be able to bounce back from a little heat wave, the cold is less forgiving, dahling, so keep your kweens feeling cozy!

As you place that hygrometer in the spot you are hoping to place that lush green gurl, look around. Is this spot close to a window, heater, or air conditioner that is going to impact the temperature of the space throughout the year? Below are some spatial thangs to keep in mind as you prepare your space to serve botanical garden realness.

WINDOWSILLS: Window areas are absolutely fabulous for our green gurls! All six windows in my lil Brooklyn apartment are filled with greenery. During the spring and summer, my kweens are loving all that warmth and sunshine, but during the fall and winter those tragic cold drafts can certainly cause plant parent struggles. Ensuring that your windows are properly insulated and moving your kweens back a few inches from the window are quick fixes!

HEATERS/AIR CONDITIONERS: While these devices can be helpful in maintaining that 65° to 75°F (18° to 24°C) situation that our green gurls enjoy, placing them too close to either of these could cause your kweens to struggle. So, whenever I turn these devices on, I make sure that my green gurls are nowhere near them.

DRAFTS: Depending on the layout of your space, you may have cold spots, hot spots, and/or drafts. Place that hygrometer in different areas of your apartment to get an idea of the various temperatures. These temperatures will change seasonally, so be sure to do a temperature check throughout the year so you know what you're working with and whether you need to move your kweens to a new, more suitable spot.

Dahling, your space is your microclimate, and if you are mindful and aware of the amount of light your space gets, the moisture in the air, and the temperature in the space, then greening up your house, apartment, or office will be a breeze! No one knows your microclimate better than you do, dahling! Strut with confidence knowing that you are informed and know how to match the needs of your future green gurls to what your space can provide.

CHAPTER 3

DECOR, DAHLING

Gurl, now that you've gotten to know your space a lil better and got those environmental factors under your belt, we can dive into some creative brainstorming to prepare your space for the arrival of your green gurls! Yas, dahling, get ready to serve interior designer realness cuz we are about to get into some chic ways to decorate so that your space is serving all kinds of viridescent vibes!

WHETHER IT WAS MY CHILDHOOD ROOM, my college dorm, or my apartment in Brooklyn, I've always enjoyed the process of making a space feel like home. She's a kween who is all about the decor. It's a key element in setting the mood, the vibe, and the overall ambiance of any space. Living in Brooklyn with over 200 green gurls in my care, I've had to be intentional and creative with how I decorate my space to ensure that it feels good for me and for my green gurls.

Sooooo, to get those creative juices flowing, I wanted to share three simple and easy planty space design ideas that I have utilized throughout the years as a plant parent.

GET THAT GREEN GURL SOME WHEELS, HUNTY!

BEING CREATIVE AND repurposing pieces of furniture to fit your botanical needs is just one of the many adventures of plant parenthood, gurl! Stumbling upon the option of using a mobile utility cart to hold some of my green gurls has been a chic little hack that has come in handy quite a bit. Being able to move a group of my green gurls around my space with ease, whether it's to temporarily make more space for myself or to let my green gurls follow the sunlight as it travels through my apartment, has been a botanical blessing.

Prior to becoming a plant parent, I never paid attention to the direction my windows faced. The sun rose and she set. I was never really concerned with the amount of sunlight that came into my space; as long as some light shone through, she was good. Early on in my plant parent journey I moved into a little prewar one-bedroom apartment. It was my third Brooklyn apartment, it was my very first time living without roommates, and a kween was excited! I was going to be able to create a home just for me and my green gurls. As I settled into the space, I took time to watch the sunlight throughout it and quickly realized that while I had west-facing windows, the enclosed courtyard that my windows faced shortened and dimmed any sunlight that shone through. The windowsills were also quite small and would not fit many of my green gurls. This kween was going to have to get creative because she was werking with a lower light situation! I ended up investing in a couple of cute modern utility carts made of metal that would allow me to roll my kweens up to the window during the brightest parts of the day and then back under a grow light during the evening as the

natural light grew dimmer. My kweens must have not minded being mobile, cuz, dahling, they grew with a fierceness for those two years I lived in that chic little spot. The lighting situation was not the best, but by being a lil creative and intentional I was able to turn a delta into a cute spatial design idea. I mean let's just admit, some indoor greenery on wheels is just a whole decor mood!

WE ALL LOVE A PLANT SHELFIE, GURL!

WHEN YOU'RE A KWEEN who has spent most of her life being about that city living, you learn that space is a commodity, and when it's limited you go vertical, gurl! Utilizing shelving has been a wonderfully simple and easy way for me to decorate my home, creating new space and transforming what would otherwise be unusable space into an area for me to display my personality and the lushness of my green gurls.

I remember when I stumbled upon my current apartment, after having looked at numerous spaces across Brooklyn. I whipped out the compass app on my phone as soon as I stepped in. South-facing windows with no obstructions, plenty of floor space, high ceilings, modern details, and wooden floors . . . gurl, it was love at first sight! Then I noticed a closed door in the living room; I thought it was another closet. I opened the door, and revealed before my eyes was a small lil nook about 45 square feet in size with south-facing windows. Gurl, I put down that deposit so quick! The apartment was mine twenty-four hours later, hunty.

The next day, I was in my new empty apartment mapping out how I was going to make this space ready for the arrival of my green little kweens. Obvi, the nook was destined to become a lil indoor greenhouse, but with its minimal floor space and bare walls I knew that adding shelves was the only way I was going to have room for any of my 100+ green gurls at the time. I went to the walls first. I used a stud finder to mark all the studs in them. These are the spots that would be my focus as I designed the layout of the shelves, as I would be anchoring the shelves into the studs to ensure that they could carry the weight of my plant fam. I went with five white fixed-bracket shelves, because white paint reflects light, making the room brighter, and the brackets provide extra support.

I focused on the floor space second. I wanted floor space to be able to meditate surrounded by the botanical magic of my green gurls. I measured the length of the floor along the east wall, where the plant stands for my green gurls would go. I went with a thin, framed, four shelf unit and two thin, framed, mini double-shelf units. The thin framed shelves would take up less space and allow more sunlight to shine through to the green gurls. I have 85 plants in that lil 45 square-foot nook, and, gurl, it's my botanical happy place!

THESE GREEN LITTLE KWEENS BE WERKS OF ART, DAHLING!

....

THERE IS SOMETHING MAGICAL about pairing the bare simplicity of blank space with the grand natural beauty that is lush greenery. Styling and letting my green gurls shine in all their glory as living, breathing art pieces in my space has been a journey of personal interior designing joy.

Being the parent of over 200 plants, I am intentional about not crowding my kweens to the point where they become an unmanageable lil jungle. I want to give them the room to spread their foliage freely, let their vines trail uninterrupted, and let their lushness radiate undisturbed, dahling. It is also helpful to not crowd your kweens too closely as this decreases the risk of spreading any pests through mere contact.

As I was decorating my bedroom in my current spot, I knew that I wanted to have a little fun with how I styled my kweens. The plant nook functioned more as an indoor greenhouse, a fabulous layout, but my main focus there was maximizing the space to fit as many green gurls as I could. I could let my creativity wander a lil more as I planned to green up my bedroom, dahling, and I was excited! I decided to go with a minimalist approach, where the largest piece of furniture in this room would be my bed, and the rest of the space would be styled with smaller decor pieces + green gurls. The east wall of this room is one of my favs! I decided to go with brass-wire shelves because they matched my bed frame (she loves a theme), they take up minimal wall space, and sunlight shines through them. This wall stands right next to a south-facing window, so I knew that the bright,

indirect light and the dapple of direct sun would be perfect for any sun-loving kween.

After figuring out the layout of where I wanted to place the shelves and marking the studs in the wall, I got to drilling, hunty! I secured the top shelf first, then started on the second right below it. As I was securing the left side of the shelf, the right side slid down the wall to create a slanted shelf situation and I fell in love with how it looked! It was a simple way to add some more flavor to the wall; it was perfection by happenstance. I treated these shelves like an art installation. The main purpose was not to get as many plants on them as possible, but to create a vibrant, living, breathing planty art wall that I could wake up to every morning.

On the west wall, I discovered that the studs in the wall were too inconsistent for any shelves to be securely mounted. So I knew that this wall was going to serve minimalist realness. I wanted a plant to go there, but I wanted a kween that made a statement! I eventually came upon my staghorn fern (Ms. *Platycerium superbum*), which is mounted on a piece of wood. I could hang this kween like the beautiful masterpiece she is!

As you plan to green up and decorate a particular spot or map out an entire area of your space, let your creative mind wander. What will maximize the use of your space while giving your green gurls the room they need to breathe, grow, and thrive? What colors, materials, and shapes will be aesthetically pleasing to your eye, while complimenting the lushness of your green gurls? How can you make this space feel like home for you and your green gurls? Take your time and let yourself ask these kinds of questions. When I was a lil younger, I used to be very quick to rush the process of decorating. I wanted to get it done and over, I wanted the space to feel like home already. Later I would regret some of my choices, because once it was done it was done, or I had to redecorate. So, gurl, take your time, be patient with yourself and all your ideas, and create the home you rightfully deserve one piece at a time.

MOUNTING A STAG-HORN FERN

DAHLING, I KNOW that for some plant parents (myself, included, gurl) ferns can be tricky kweens to care for . . . but, gurl, staghorn ferns are green gurls near and dear to my heart! I welcomed my very first staghorn fern into my plant fam about three years ago. It is embedded in a coconut shell. My second staghorn fern is the kween mounted on wood, and this kween was obsessed!

Ms. Staghorn Fern (Ms. *Platycerium bifurcatum,* if you wanna get fancy) belongs to the genus *Platycerium* and is native to tropical regions of Africa, Southeast Asia, and Australia, where she grows on trees as an epiphyte. Epiphytes are green gurls that grow on the surface of other plants and trees, deriving moisture and nutrients from the air, rain, water (in marine situations), or from debris accumulating around them. I've found this kween to be hearty, and resilient to my plant kween newbie mistakes back in the day!

I've always kept my staghorn kweens in very bright, indirect light, having learned that direct sunlight can burn their lush green leaves (the antler fronds).

When it comes to watering, I either let the entire plant soak in my sink until saturated or let her sit in the shower for a bit with room-temp water for a couple of minutes. I've found it important to let her brown set of leaves (the shield fronds) soak completely, as their function is to protect the plant roots, and take up water and nutrients. She enjoys high humidity, so any bright bathroom would be perfect for her. If she's in a less humid spot, I mist her twice a week, focusing on the underside of the antler fronds and the shield fronds.

I've seen staghorn ferns sold in pots, but because these kweens are epiphytes, mature staghorn kweens should be mounted on a board or hung in a hanging basket, as this mimics how they would be growing if they were in their natural habitat.

So let's sink our roots into a lil activity so that your staghorn fern kween is serving all kinds of wall art realness!

MATERIALS YOU'LL NEED, GURL!

1 potted staghorn fern

1 bag of sphagnum moss

1 pencil

3 to 5 feet of twine

Rot-resistant wood board

Picture wire or hanging bracket + screws + screwdriver

8 small nails + hammer

TIP: When it comes to choosing your wooden board, you have a variety of options before you, which can be overwhelming! I would focus on two thangs: the size of the board and the wood it's made of. While ferns are slow growers, they can reach quite a grand size with a lil TLC. The larger the board you start with, the longer your green gurl will grow undisturbed. Additionally, the wood should be rot-resistant, because you will be soaking this kween in water from time to time and you do not want rotten wood on your wall, gurl. Oak, hickory, pecan, manzanita, cedar, redwood, cypress, and Douglas fir bark are great rot-resistant choices!

STEP 1
GETTING THAT GREEN GURL READY!

First thang first, dahling: Let's get that green gurl out of her nursery pot! Massage some of that old soil away and loosen up her roots so that you're left with about an inch or so of soil attached to the base of the plant. Make note of the size of the base of this green gurl and her brown shield fronds, which will help you with measuring

thangs out in the next couple of steps. Place that green gurl to the side; it's time to get to werk on her new home.

STEP 2
PREP THAT BOARD, HUNTY!

Let's get that hanging bracket or picture wire that will attach to the wall onto the back of your wooden board. Make sure that the hanging device of your choice is the

appropriate size for the weight of your growing green gurl and her new wooden home. Flip the board over and use your pencil to trace a circle on the board that's at least an inch wider than the base of your green gurl. Next, grab those nails and hammer in the eight small nails around the edge of the circle; depending on the size of your circle, you may need more or fewer nails. These nails will secure your green gurl to her new home.

3

4

STEP 3
BRING THEM TOGETHA, DAHLING!

Now it's time to introduce this green gurl to her new home! Take a bit of damp sphagnum moss to create a little moss bed between the board and the plant in the middle of the nails. Place the base of your green gurl on that moss bed, and lightly secure it to the board using twine. Grab some more damp moss and wrap it around the base of that kween to cover and contain any dirt and roots. Once she's fully wrapped with moss, wrap the moss with the twine thoroughly, connecting with the nails in all directions. Do not cover the shield fronds, just gently lift them and go underneath. This twine is the only thang keeping the masterpiece together so make sure to hit every nail.

STEP 4
SHE'S READY FOR HER CLOSE-UP!

After you have secured that green gurl to her new home, gently lift her vertically to make sure that thangs are properly attached. Let any of that loose soil or moss fall to the ground, and if she does not budge, then, dahling, she's ready! Get a nail into the wall you plan to place her on, hang her up, and let her lushness shine!

CHAPTER 4

RESEARCHING THAT GREEN GURL

I remember when I was a newbie plant parent just beginning on my botanical journey, building my plant fam with such eagerness and excitement! My very first plant, my Marble Queen pothos (Ms. *Epipremnum aureum*), was growing with a lushness and I figured if I could get this one kween to thrive, then I could get any green gurl to thrive! She was feeling confident!

"Take a look at her nursery pot to check and see if you can find her name, and the research begins."

I WOULD HOP ON MY LIL BIKE and ride around Brooklyn, having mapped out a list of all the plant shops I wanted to visit the night before, and I would strut into those nurseries and pick up any plant that caught my eye. No research of any kind was involved, gurl. If her foliage was fierce, lush, and she could fit in my apartment, I was sold; that plant was coming home with me. This resulted in a kween purchasing plants that 1) I did not know how to care for because I was unaware of their specific plant care needs; 2) were simply too difficult for this plant parent newbie to care for at the time; and 3) weren't a match for the current environmental conditions in my apartment. Many of my green gurls were not happy with me during the beginning of this wild plant parent journey, hunty! And yas, gurl, there were botanical casualties.

So, kween, as you dive into the lush adventure of getting your space to serve all kinds of botanical realness, learn a lil somethang somethang from my newbie plant parent mistakes and DO YOUR RESEARCH!

Researching the green gurl you hope to welcome into your space is crucial in ensuring that you can provide that green little kween with everything she needs to grow and thrive! And, gurl, I am here to help! Take a look at her nursery pot to check and see if you can find her name, and the research begins. What's the environment like in this kween's native home? How much sunlight does this green gurl enjoy? Does she prefer drier soil, or is she a kween that needs frequent watering? Is humidity a thang this kween needs to keep looking lush? Answering these questions will let you know whether your home can provide this kween with a scene she will enjoy.

Here are eight of my favorite green gurls for beginner plant parents!

1 THE SNAKE PLANT (Ms. *Dracaena trifasciata*)

NATIVE TO PARTS OF AFRICA, Madagascar, and southern Asia with over seventy different fabulous varieties, the snake plant has easily become one of my favorite green gurls! These extremely resilient, adaptable, and easy-to-care-for kweens can grow anywhere from 8 inches to 12 feet high in their natural habitat. My tallest snake plant is actually taller than me! Their sword-like foliage is simply fierce and can range from dark green with yellow striping (*Dracaena trifasciata* 'Laurentii') to a pale green variegated with hints of white (*Dracaena* 'Sayuri'). It is what drew me to this kween in the first place. Historically, these kweens have been cherished in Chinese, African, Japanese, and Brazilian cultures. In China, it was believed that the eight gods showered their virtues (long life, prosperity, intelligence, beauty, art, poetry, health, and strength) onto those who grew these green gurls. In parts of Africa, this kween has even been used for medicinal purposes and as a protective charm against bewitchment.

Ms. Snake Plant is also known for being one of the top air-purifying plants. Studies, including those performed by NASA, have consistently shown this kween to remove toxins such as formaldehyde and benzene from the air. Yas, hunty, this kween has quite the reputation.

LIGHT
While these kweens can be quite adaptable to a myriad of lighting situations, I find that they thrive in bright, indirect light with some direct sun. If you are werking with a dimmer lighting situation, don't fret, dahling, these kweens can adapt to it.

WATER
These kweens are succulents and they are fabulous at storing water in their roots and hardy leaves, which act like a reservoir for her to draw on to quench her thirst. Letting these kweens dry out between waterings is key to ensuring that they do not experience root rot. I water these green gurls every 7 to 10 days in the warmer months and every 3 to 4 weeks in the winter months.

SOIL
Well-drained, well-aerated, loose soil is this kween's scene. I use a 50% potting soil, 25% fir bark, 25% perlite mixture that helps the water drain through the soil quickly, ensuring that this kween is not sitting in moist soil for too long.

2 THE POTHOS (Ms. *Epipremnum aureum*)

NATIVE TO CHINA, the Indian subcontinent, Australia, New Guinea, Southeast Asia, and various islands of the Pacific and Indian Oceans with over fifty varieties, the pothos ivy is a tropical kween that is near and dear to my heart, and was the first green gurl I ever welcomed into my Brooklyn home! Though pothos are popular in temperate regions, their ability to survive in a myriad of environments has led to their becoming naturalized in tropical and subtropical forests worldwide. In ideal conditions, various varieties of these vigorous vining kweens can grow 20 to 65 feet high and 3 to 6 feet wide, with their leaves growing up to 30 inches long! And speaking of their lush leaves, they can range from green with yellow variegation (golden pothos) to bright lime green (neon pothos) to green with white variegation (Marble Queen pothos). Yas, gurl, these kweens have range!

Ms. Pothos has been nicknamed the devil's vine or devil's ivy because of her seemingly supernatural "hard-to-kill" resilience, and she's known to stay lush in the dimmest of lighting situations. She's a survivor and there ain't no denying it!

LIGHT

While these kweens are quite resilient and adaptable to a lower light scene, I've found that good ole bright, indirect light is the best way to go. Variegated varieties of these kweens may revert back to an all-green lewk if they aren't given enough sunshine, but simply moving them to a brighter situation should restore that variegation, dahling. Pale leaves can mean that she is getting too much sun and may need shadier conditions to serve that lush lewk once again.

WATER

Like most of my green gurls, I let these kweens dry out in between waterings to avoid root rot, which could look like black spots on the leaves or yellowing leaves that eventually drop off. While you can check the soil to see if the plants need water, these kweens are very good at telling you when they need a drink, as they start to wilt when they are thirsty. I water these kweens once a week during the warmer months and every 2 weeks in those colder months.

SOIL

Interestingly, I've seen these kweens thrive in a container with water for months, but I like to have my pothos green gurls' roots grounded in soil to ensure they can get the nutrients they need to keep lewking lush. I tend to go with a 75% potting soil, 25% perlite mix for these kweens to make sure the soil is well drained. If you ever find that the water sits at the top of the soil for too long, take a chopstick and poke some holes in the soil to let some air reach those roots.

3 THE ZZ PLANT (Ms. *Zamioculcas zamiifolia*)

LIGHT

With her chlorophyll-packed leaves, this green gurl can survive in a wide range of lighting situations, which makes her a fierce kween for multiple indoor spaces. I tend to keep her in bright, indirect light with very little to no direct sun, as direct sun could cause sunburn and we ain't about that life! And just a lil tip, dahling: When her leaves start to look a lil dull and dusty, wipe them off with a damp cloth. Her leaves are her meal ticket and less dust equals more sunshine for this kween to make the energy she needs to grow and thrive.

NATIVE TO EASTERN AFRICA, from southern Kenya to northeastern South Africa, this now popular indoor tropical kween was probably not known to anyone outside the continent of Africa before 1996. She grew outdoors in all kinds of lush ways for years, but it wasn't until then that Dutch nurseries located in South Africa, which saw her propagating potential, started distributing this kween all around the world. And it comes as no surprise that she has easily traveled the globe because she is so low maintenance and easy to care for! She was the third plant I ever bought and even through my tragic mistakes as an amateur plant kween back in tha day, she still survived and thrived! And yes, hunty, she is still alive and well these four years later!

With her naturally glossy dark green leaves, this kween can grow up to 4 feet tall, and spread out 4 feet wide at maturity when grown indoors under ideal conditions. And while she is notorious for being a kween that takes her time when it comes to pushing out that new growth, I've met plant parents who've had their green gurl for over thirty years, still serving lush lewks as if she was a young leafling! She ages well, and she ain't afraid to show it!

WATER

ZZ plants grow from large, thick rhizomes that resemble potatoes. Rhizomes are subterranean plant stems that are often thickened by deposits of reserve food material. In short, these rhizomes store water, which is why this green gurl does well during droughts and in the houses of plant parents on the go, who occasionally forget to water their green gurls. While these kweens are tropical, I tend to water them like I do my succulents, every 7 to 10 days in the warmer months and every 3 to 4 weeks in the winter months. Let that soil dry out in between waterings; when in doubt it is always better to under-water these kweens than over-water!

SOIL

While these kweens are not picky about their soil mixture, I use my 50% potting soil, 25% fir bark, 25% perlite mixture which helps the water drain through the soil quickly, ensuring that this kween is not sitting in moist soil for too long. I've also seen some plant parents use sphagnum peat moss, organic compost, and sterilized loam in their soil mixture.

4 THE RUBBER TREE (Ms. *Ficus elastica*)

NATIVE TO EASTERN PARTS of South Asia and Southeast Asia, this durable, sturdy, and resilient kween has also become naturalized in Sri Lanka, the West Indies, and the US state of Florida. While her nickname, rubber tree, may be intriguing, she is neither made of rubber nor used for it now (in the early 1900s a low grade of rubber was made from the white sticky sap harvested from her trunk and stems). When I first heard her Latin name, *Ficus elastica*, I fell in love. It sounded like the name of a drag queen I wanted to meet! *Ficus*, referring to the fig-like fruits that grow in pairs along her mature branches, and *elastica* referring to the white sticky sap. While indoors she can grow up to a cute 10 feet tall, in her natural environment she can grow into an evergreen shrub or tree that may grow 50 to 100 feet tall with a fabulously gargantuan canopy of draping, foot-long oval, glossy leaves and lengthy dangling aerial roots.

When I was in Cuba a few years ago, I remember looking up at a huge tree and being absolutely shook—it was Ms. *Ficus elastica* herself! I was so used to seeing smaller versions of her that she took me by surprise when I saw her true growth potential! This experience was a reminder that most of the green gurls we bring into our homes are just small leaflings whose origins stem from massive, majestic green kweens.

LIGHT

This kween is a green gurl who knows her scene and it's the brightest spot you can find, with little to no direct light. Direct sunlight could result in sunburned leaves, and too little light could cause her to lose her lower leaves and have the remaining ones go dull. I've found that she really enjoys my south-facing windows paired with a sheer curtain to filter the light. I've also grown these kweens in lower light conditions with the help of a full-spectrum grow light.

WATER

When this kween is pushing out that new growth during the summer, I find that she enjoys her roots being fully soaked with that delicious H_2O. I tend to let the faucet run over her soil for a minute or two, letting the water run through her planter's drainage hole. During the winter months, I do not soak her, but I am making sure that her soil does not completely dry out. I tend to keep this kween in a plastic planter with drainage holes, as this type of planter retains more moisture in between waterings. I water this kween once a week during her growing season (warmer months) and every 10 to 14 days when she is dormant (colder months). Check the top inch of her soil: if it's dry, she needs a drank, and if it's damp, her thirst is quenched!

SOIL

Well-drained soil is the way to go! I do a 75% potting soil and 25% fir bark mixture, as this helps to ensure that the soil stays a bit damp after a good watering, but not soggy. Soggy soil will cause this kween to experience root rot, and we ain't got time for that!

5 THE SPIRAL CACTUS (Ms. *Cereus forbesii* 'Spiralis')

THOUGHT TO BE A CLONE derived from vegetative propagation of the original green gurl discovered in South America (in parts of Peru, Brazil, and Argentina), this quirky cactus stands out from the bunch by serving all kinds of twist-and-turn realness with her blue-green color and spiraling, columnar form. It is said that around the 1980s a few branches from the original kween were imported in Europe. The original cactus was characterized by strong gray stems covered with a dense whitish powdery coating; however, all the kweens that now grace our homes with their fierce and funky presence are most likely hybrid specimens grown from seed derived from cross-pollination, probably with *Cereus peruvianus* or *Cereus stenogonus*. Dahling, our green gurls have quite the story when you look at their history.

These kweens' spirals typically begin to develop when they reach the height of 3 to 4 inches. In her natural environment, this kween can reach heights of 8 to 13 feet and taller, gurl, growing numerous columnar, spiral stems branching at the base in a candelabra-like situation. And while this sturdy and easy-to-care-for kween may have a tough exterior with her sharp spines, in summer months under the right conditions she blooms beautiful white and pink flowers that when pollinated produce large purplish ornamental fruit. She's not a one-trick pony, dahling. Get into it!

LIGHT
When she is a lil young cactus kween, she prefers light shade, with bright, indirect light and no direct light. However, when she matures, she prefers brighter light with some full sun. And just a note, dahling: While cacti and succulents love that bright light, hunty, exposing them to too much full sun can actually burn some of these green gurls. I've always made the assumption that the more full sun the better, but this is not always the case!

WATER
Water these kweens according to the season, gurl! During the warmer months, these green gurls are thriving and drinking up much more water than when they're resting in the colder months. During colder months, I water these kweens every 3 to 4 weeks. During the warmer months, I water them every 1 to 2 weeks, and I make sure that the water evenly soaks the soil!

SOIL
Soil matters, dahling! I have my spiral cactus potted in a 40% potting soil, 25% perlite, 25% fir bark, 10% sand mixture as this ensures that the soil drains faster and prevents over-watering!

6 THE JADE PLANT (Ms. *Crassula ovata*)

NATIVE TO THE DESERT REGIONS of KwaZulu-Natal and Eastern Cape Provinces of South Africa and to Mozambique, this hardy succulent is all about those lush vibes and good juju! She's a kween that goes by many names, dahling: money tree, lucky plant, friendship tree, pink joy, or dollar plant cuz she is said to invite good fortune and luck into any home she enters, according to the feng shui. This traditional practice originating in ancient China says that placement is key, and the jade plant brings different energies depending on where you place her. In east locations she's bringing family harmony, health, initiation of projects, and scholarly pursuits. Situated in a southeast situation she's bringing that wealth luck. West locations are for that good creativity. And in northwest situations, she's bringing those good vibes when it comes to your area of werk. Yas, this green gurl has a multitude of vibes.

In their natural habitats (dry, rocky hillsides) these kweens with their thick woody stems and smooth, shiny, plump green leaves can grow 8 to 9 feet tall, as rounded shrubs. Indoors, with a cute ideal scene, time, and patience these green girls can grow up to 5 feet. They are often trimmed when indoors to resemble chic lil trees, and, dahling, I'm here for it! In her natural habitat (or an indoor mimic) this kween blooms starry white to pink flowers.

LIGHT

When these kweens are young, the ideal sunlight situation is bright, indirect light, since long periods of direct sun can cause sunburn, and their leaves are too cute for that, dahling. However, when these kweens are mature, they thrive with a few hours of fun sun each day. Four hours of direct sun seems to be the magic number for my jade plants. When these green gurls do not get enough sun, their growth is stunted and their stems become leggy.

WATER

Jade plants are succulents, so they are built to retain water in their leaves, roots, and stems, to get them through droughts and dry spells. When these kweens are growing (spring and summer), I tend to water them once a week, making sure I soak the soil and let it dry out just a bit before giving them another drink. During the winter months, when this kween is dormant, I water these green gurls every 2 to 3 weeks, making sure the soil is completely dried out in between waterings. Gurl, I've even heard that some larger and more mature jades may need only one to two waterings throughout the winter.

SOIL

I use my standard 50% potting soil, 25% fir bark, 25% perlite succulent soil mixture for these kweens and they love it! The soil should be well drained and aerated to ensure that the roots are not sitting wet or soggy for too long.

7 THE AIR PLANT (Ms. *Tillandsia*)

NATIVE TO THE FORESTS, mountains, and deserts of the West Indies, Mexico, Central America, South America, and the southernmost border states of the United States, this otherworldly green gurl with over five hundred varieties is one intriguing kween! Under most conditions, not needing soil for growth, air plants are epiphytic in nature. Epiphytes are green gurls that grow on the surface of other plants and trees, deriving moisture and nutrients from the air, rain, water (in marine situations), or from debris accumulating around them. Their leaves, ranging from a bright dusty green to a fuzzy silvery sage, are often covered with trichomes capable of absorbing all the delicious H_2O that gathers on them. Mesic air plants have smoother, greener foliage (fewer trichomes) and are typically in environments with a moderate level of humidity. Xeric air plants be serving that fuzzy gray realness (more trichomes) and are often found in drier, desert climates. The drier the environment, the better these kweens need to be at catching the moisture in the air around them, and more trichomes help them do just that.

These slow-growing kweens often form a rosette pattern with new growth appearing from the center, and when under ideal conditions will bloom a colorful tubular-shaped flower. In the wild some of these kweens can grow up to 3 feet long, or be found in large clumps of multiple plants. Individually, these kweens are of a quaint size, easily fitting in your hand, and are fabulous green gurls to diversify the greenery in your home.

LIGHT
Bright, indirect light is this kween's scene. A good thing to keep in mind: the higher the humidity in your space, the more light that kween will welcome into her life. I tend to have my air plants in my sunny bathroom window, and they are thriving with all kinds of new growth realness. For anyone with lower light situations, these kweens can also survive with full-spectrum grow lights!

WATER
Watering these kweens is simple, dahling! Fill up that bowl or container with lukewarm/room-temperature water—rainwater, aquarium water, or pond water is best because they are richer in those nutrients these kweens love. I tend to stay away from tap water, as city tap water has fewer minerals and nutrients, so I use spring water instead. Submerge the entire green gurl, and let her soak for 20 to 30 minutes. Afterward, place that kween on a dish towel upside down to ensure that there isn't any water trapped in between her leaves; let her dry completely. I tend to soak these kweens about once a week, with a daily misting.

SOIL
She doesn't need any, dahling!

8 THE HEARTLEAF PHILODENDRON
(Ms. *Philodendron scandens*)

NATIVE TO TROPICAL RAINFORESTS, swamps, and riverbanks of Mexico, Brazil, and the West Indies, these climbing vine kweens with their glossy, green heart-shaped leaves are simply sweethearts! And don't let her name fool you, dahling, cuz she is tough as nails. In the wild, you'll find this green gurl climbing the trunks and branches of trees, reaching from the forest floor to the sunlight above the lush canopy using those hardy aerial roots to cling to the bark. The name derives from the Greek: *philo* meaning "love" or "affection" and *dendron* meaning "tree," which basically translates to "tree hugger," gurl.

Indoors, I've found this kween to be quite resilient, durable, and all about that lush growth! While these kweens will do perfectly fine in a hanging basket, letting their lush vines dangle in the air, I find that heartleaf philodendrons enjoy a moss pole situation. A moss pole is a very simple concept: start with some kind of stake—bamboo, wood scrap, or even plastic—and wrap it in moss. You can have a lil DIY moment and make one or find one at your local plant shop. Moss poles mimic their natural habitat, and I've found that kweens with moss poles tend to produce larger leaves than their hanging basket sisters. While these green gurls are of tropical origin, they are tolerant of drier air! I mist the moss pole these kweens cling to, just to make sure those aerial roots are able to get a lil drink.

LIGHT

This kween loves a bright, indirect lighting situation but can survive in lower lighting! I have also used full-spectrum grow lights, and this kween was here for the fluorescent vibe, dahling! If she is not getting enough light, her stems will become leggy and her foliage won't look as vibrant and glossy.

WATER

This tropical kween loves a humid and moist soil situation! In the warmer months I water once a week, trying to keep her soil damp, but not soggy, which will cause root rot. A little trick I often do to make sure that she does not dry out completely for long periods of time is placing her in a plastic planter with drainage instead of my go-to terra-cotta pot. Plastic pots hold and keep moisture, which this kween prefers. In the colder months, I water this kween every 10 to 14 days to ensure that this dormant kween is drying out slightly in between waterings. Yellow leaves can be a sign of root rot, while dry brown leaves can mean she wants a cute glass of H_2O.

SOIL

Well-drained soil is my go-to for this kween! A mix of 75% potting soil and 25% fir bark works perfectly. The higher percentage of soil helps to keep some of the moisture, while the fir bark helps to ensure that air is reaching the roots and preventing root rot.

Plants
Make
People
Happy.®
Maximum of five people in line at one time.
Open
Monday–Saturday
12-8pm
Sundays
12-7pm

LET'S GO PLANT SHOPPING!

Gurl, give yoself a pat on your shoulder cuz you have reached chapter 5 of this lil botanical journey and you are well on your way to becoming that plant parent serving all kinds of viridescent vibes, botanical realness, and lush lewks!

LET'S RECOUNT THE STEPS you've taken so far! You've looked within yourself, preparing your inner being for the beauty that is plant parenthood, cuz we throwing all those pre-plant-parent jitters out the window. You've done your research on your space, so that you know what kind of scene you're bringing your green little kweens into. You've brainstormed decor ideas and how you are going to get that spot or space ready for the arrival of your green gurls. And you've got a cute list of some fabulous kweens that are perfect for any beginner plant parent. Dahling, you are ready for one of my absolutely fav thangs to do: PLANT SHOPPING!

And because she is a kween who is all about a routine, I thought I'd share four easy steps I tend to find myself doing when I'm treating myself to some botanical retail therapy.

STEP 1
PERUSE THE SHOP, DAHLING.

You may already have a green gurl in mind, or perhaps you are living on the wild side and having a lil spontaneous plant shopping date with yourself. Either way, allow yourself to soak up all that greenery and explore the shop's selection of those green little kweens. Take your time, jam to some music on those headphones, and take note of any green gurls that catch your eye. Enjoy this process, relish the mini lil jungle around you—you deserve it, gurl!

STEP 2
IDENTIFY THAT GREEN GURL.

Now that you have a good idea of the plant selection in the shop, it's time to dive into those green gurls that caught your eye. Pick that kween up and take a look at her nursery pot to see if you can find her Latin name or nickname. If you've already done your research and you know the general care tips for that kween, then you've found your green gurl! If you don't know anything about the plant you just picked up, then whip out that phone and google it! Type in the name of the kween followed by "indoor care tips." You'll find a flood of various links, click the first few, and read through to get a general idea of who this kween is and what kind of scene she thrives in. This process will provide you with enough information to figure out if that green gurl is a match for you and your space.

STEP 3
INSPECT THOSE LEAVES AND THAT SOIL.

Now that you've matched up with your green gurl, it's time to make sure this is a healthy kween. Take a look at the leaves: Are they yellowing, are they dry or brittle, are there any pests crawling around, is there any fungus or bacteria growing, are they wilting? If the answer is yes to any of these thangs, then you may want to go with another green gurl. I also tend to check the soil, just to make sure there are no weeds growing or pests crawling around. Make sure you are welcoming a lush, healthy, pest-free plant into your home. Any new growth is a good sign that that green gurl is growing and ready to expand her roots. If you do find any plants with pests, let the shopkeeper know; they will appreciate you for it.

Pick your plant, pick your planter.

STEP 4
PAIR THAT KWEEN WITH A PLANTER, HUNTY.

You have your lush green gurl, and now it's time to find her a planter that she can sink her roots into! Make sure that the pot is at least 2 inches larger than her nursery pot, cuz we want that kween to have some room to grow! We'll get into some of my fav kinds of pots and planters in the next chapter, dahling.

When I started out on this journey, five years ago, I had no idea that there was such a beautiful local community of plant shops and nurseries in Brooklyn. I had defaulted to buying my very first plant from a local hardware store that happened to have plants outside its storefront. I knew that there had to be more local options where I could explore my newfound green passion. I was on a mission to find more plant shops and nurseries in my borough. So, gurl, she Google-Mapped it! I typed in "plant shops" and, boom, I had a running list of lush spots I needed to visit. And so, on the weekends I would hop on my bike and have lil botanical Brooklyn adventures, visiting the different plant shops and nurseries on my ever-growing list. I encourage you to do the same. Do a lil search of the shops and nurseries that are in your area!

One of the many things I love about all the plant shops and nurseries I frequent is that each one has its own personality and vibe. Each one feeds my plant parent experience in a different way. As you begin to build your own lil lush list of shops, you'll find that each shop will nurture the plant parent in you in various ways. Here are some plant shops and nurseries that I have spent countless weekends blissfully wandering, picking out green gurls to welcome into my home, and what I love about each one of these botanical havens.

CREST
HARDWARE
& URBAN
GARDEN
CENTER

SERVING LOCAL
BOTANICAL ESCAPE

@cresthardware

We all need those spaces that transport you. When you bring your being and bawdy into that space, you feel as if you have escaped the hecticness of your city, your town, your neighborhood . . . the space brings a sense of peacefulness, calmness, and just plain ole happiness, dahling. Well, Crest Hardware & Urban Garden Center is that spot for me!

LOCATED IN WILLIAMSBURG, BROOKLYN, this botanical beauty of a shop is truly a hidden gem. I remember walking through the front doors of Crest for the first time and feeling a bit puzzled because it looked like a standard hardware store at first. This spot had been on my list for a while and a few of my plant frands had raved about the nursery the store had, so I was bubbling with a botanical eagerness to experience the lushness my frands could not stop talking about. I went over to the register and asked the store clerk where the nursery was. They pointed to the back of the store and I skipped right on over! Dahling, when I opened that door and stepped inside it felt like I had been transported to a lil lush haven! Crest is one of my favorites because the vibe, warmth, and coziness of its wooden greenhouse makes my soul happy. The way the sun shines through the transparent ceiling, hitting the wooden shelves, terra-cotta pots, and lush greenery is just a whole mood and has served as a major decor inspiration for me. She's all about pairing warm colors with the viridescent lushness of her green gurls.

The organization of the greenhouse makes the plant shopping experience easy and effortless. Plants are grouped by lighting needs, so I can go to a section of the greenhouse and already have a good sense of what a particular green gurl needs to thrive just by where she is placed in the shop! This is fabulous for beginner plant parents who may be a bit overwhelmed by all the lushness.

After opening Crest Hardware in 1962, Manny Franquinha became an icon in the Brooklyn neighborhood of Williamsburg through his dedication to customer service and focus on community improvement. His son, Joseph Franquinha, continues the Crest legacy, and their lush botanical escape of a shop has never looked greener!

SOME LUSH TAKEAWAYS

→ Look out for plant shops that organize their green gurls by their sunlight needs. This is super helpful for any plant parent when choosing the next green gurl to welcome into the plant fam!

→ When plant shopping, soak up those botanical feelz and let the ambiance of the shop take you away to your own lil lush escape. The shopping experience should be a calming and enjoyable one.

GREENERY
UNLIMITED

SERVING BIOPHILIC
DESIGN REALNESS

@greeneryunlimited

Dahling, this kween is all about structural designs that intentionally incorporate the beauty of greenery—the possibilities are limitless (or should I say unlimited!). I've always admired various exterior structures, interior designs, and layouts that are strategically built to uplift and coexist with nature. I had never seen this so beautifully integrated into the design of a plant shop until I pranced on over to Greenery Unlimited.

LOCATED IN GREENPOINT, Brooklyn, this inspiring store is one of the world's first biophilic design plant shops. The theory of biophilia suggests that humans have a deep connection to the natural world and experience greater well-being when in and around the lushness of nature. Biologist Edward O. Wilson introduced and popularized the hypothesis in his book *Biophilia*, and defined it as "the urge to affiliate with other forms of life." Biophilic design applies the principles of biophilia to human spaces such as homes and offices, employing nature's beneficial and restorative experience indoors. This shop is more than just a traditional plant store serving green gurl realness; it also provides systems to keep plants alive and thriving, such as grow lighting, irrigation systems, specialty vessels, and tools, dahling. One of the fierce green installations and biophilic design concepts that I love about this shop is its 120-square-foot lush green gurl wall. And don't even get me started on the cute central seating area with a self-contained irrigation and fertilization system supporting a 12-fabulous-foot *Ficus* tree. The shop even has a pressurized misting hub that creates a chic cloud forest-like atmosphere throughout the day . . . dahling, it's a whole mood. I've also found myself playing around with the interactive digital display that offers detailed plant care guides and serves as a way for plant parents like myself to continue to learn about the various green gurls in stock and systems in the shop.

While house plants have been growing in popularity, Rebecca Bullene and Adam Besheer, owners of Greenery Unlimited, have been simultaneously focusing on developing systems to automate plant care and simplifying horticultural tools to make them more accessible to everyone, hunty!

SOME LUSH TAKEAWAYS

→ Let your local plant shops botanically inspire you! The fusion of interior and exterior design and nature so wonderfully curated by Greenery Unlimited has inspired my future home designs for sure!

→ Get to know the plant shop owners, cuz they be a wealth of knowledge. Any convo I've had with Rebecca and Adam, I've always learned something new!

We don't see plants as a trend. Nature is essential to human well-being and productivity, and we want to provide the knowledge and tools that will allow people to incorporate more nature into their daily lives. By creating a space dedicated to biophilic design principles, we hope to foster conversations and inspire others to consider how they can incorporate nature in meaningful ways into their living and working spaces.

—REBECCA BULLENE
AND ADAM BESHEER

TULA PLANTS
AND DESIGN

SERVING DESERT OASIS CHIC

:camera: @tulahouse

I love a shop that radiates an ambiance, a unique vibe, and is designed to spark a sense of creativity! I often find myself taking a mental note of the decor, wall colors, furniture, and shelving when I am in a plant shop that I love and adore for my own interior design inspirations, and Tula Plants and Design is one of those shops!

WITH ITS FAB RED WALLS, chic green-tiled plant shower, spiral staircase, and high ceilings, Tula is basically serving lewks of the loft apartment of my dreams! I fell in love with the design and layout of the space the moment I stepped inside. The showroom displays a wonderful variety of tropical green gurls and has a station where you can mix and make your own potting soil recipe. The west room of the shop is one of my absolute favorites, the arid room! This lil desert oasis of a room displays a collection of extraordinary cacti and succulent species, ranging from Ms. *Cereus forbesii* 'Spiralis' (the spiral cactus) to Ms. *Myrtillocactus geometrizans* 'Fukurokuryuzinboku' (the boob cactus). Some of the cacti and succulents I've seen on their shelves are species I've never seen in person before, making my inner plant nerd jump for joy. I often find myself having conversations with the knowledgeable shopkeepers about the various care tips and the best potting soil mixture for these prickly green gurls when I am looking to welcome a new plant into my home.

Since Tula launched in 2016, Christan Summers and Ivan Martinez, co-founders of Tula House, have cultivated wonderful relationships with growers from all over the world, who have welcomed them into their fabulous greenhouses, and shared with them their robust plant knowledge. The experience of sharing knowledge—from grower to grower, year over year, century over century—is embedded in Tula's ethos and it's one of the reasons I love this shop.

SOME LUSH TAKEAWAYS

→ Find that plant shop that keeps you coming back for more! Tula is one that has consistently impressed me with its wild variety of green gurls, one of the reasons I adore it. When it comes to cacti and succulents, I know that I can count on this shop!

→ Let the plant shops you find serve as potential decor inspiration. Tula is my apartment decor inspiration and feeds me a good dose of creativity every time I visit. If you find a plant shop that does the same, hold on to it, dahling!

THE SILL

SERVING MODERN PLANT
SHOP FABULOSITY

📷 @thesill

Gurl, you gotta love a plant shop serving a modern mewd, and The Sill is just that. With a focus on making the plant shopping experience as seamless as possible, it fuses the best parts of grandma's garden supply center (the green gurls) and creates an effortless shopping experience (without getting those hands too dirty, gurl).

I FOUND THIS CHIC SHOP during one of my werk lunch break struts through my office's neighborhood. I walked in and I fell in love with the minimalist, chic decor and maximalist plant parent energy the spot was serving. It was such a pleasant surprise to find green gurls perfect for city living that were just the right size for my windowsill. While this kween loves herself a larger plant, sometimes I like to test out my plant parent skills on smaller green gurls before committing to welcoming a larger version of the kween into my home. Since first encountering the shop, I now regularly pop by The Sill during the werk day to get a lil dose of the botanical retail therapy.

Eliza Blank launched The Sill exclusively online in 2012, and since then has opened shops in Manhattan, Brooklyn, Los Angeles, and San Francisco. You best believe that this kween will be visiting those West Coast shops as soon as she gets the chance! Plants make people happy, dahling, and The Sill is all about making that botanical happiness evergreen.

SOME LUSH TAKEAWAYS

→ It be about the shopping experience! I love a plant shop that makes the green gurl shopping experience seamless, easy, and effortless! This should be a fun process for you, not a stressful one, dahling.

→ Sometimes you stumble upon fabulous plant shops just by walking around your neighborhood, so go explore!

In January 2020, we opened the doors to the fifth Sill shop in Cobble Hill, Brooklyn. We've been rooted in NYC since opening our Lower East Side shop in 2015, and we are beyond excited to now be a part of the Brooklyn plant community. Our shops feature a selection of easy-care houseplants, along with a collection of specialty plants that rotate weekly. You just pick your plant and pick your planter! We'll even pot it right on the spot for you.

—ELIZA BLANK

HORTI

SERVING A PLAYFUL
BOTANICAL WONDERLAND

@ *@heyhorti*

Horti has been my magical botanical playground since our first social media collaboration, a place where I've been able to explore so many aspects of being a plant parent and just the Brooklyn botanical scene in general.

WHETHER THROUGH conversations about self-care, community care, or brainstorming innovative ways to continue to build with each other; or in the wild insights into the behind-the-scenes of the green gurl market; or in dreaming up fabulous initiatives to aid folks in effortlessly greening up their lives; or by trying the subscription model as a new way of welcoming green gurls into my home . . . I've simply been blessed to grow with and learn so much from this fabulous team of dedicated plant parents.

Prior to meeting my Horti fam, I'd never heard of nor been a part of a plant subscription sish. It was just a new concept for the plant parent newbie at the time, dahling, but I was eager to explore it! I remember going on a lil plant nursery adventure with Puneet Sabharwal and Bryana Sortino, co-founders of Horti, as they stocked up on plants that would be shipped out to their subscribers. The love, care, and attention that they put into selecting each and every green gurl that would eventually be sent all over the country was inspiring. After ensuring that those selected green gurls were serving all kinds of healthy, lush realness, I knew that the green gurl that would eventually be delivered to my doorstep (yas,

gurl, she be a subscriber) would have been chosen with that plant parent kind of care, and that this would ring true for all the folks who are a part of the Hey Horti community.

So, dahling, if you want a lil green surprise to pop up at your doorstep every month paired with the tools, support, and community to aid you in your own growth as a plant parent and the growth of your green gurls, check out my favs at HeyHorti.com.

SOME LUSH TAKEAWAYS

→ Build relationships with your local plant shops and enjoy the botanical ride of building with and supporting each other! Explore and see what community initiatives your local plants shops are nurturing and get involved!

→ Let your plant shops introduce you to new ways of building your plant fam! I had never explored the subscription model prior to Horti, and now I look forward to my monthly planty delivery!

We don't just want to push you plants: we want to help you realize how easy it can be to take care of them. Plants are an intimate part of our lives—we live with them and love them every day—and we want to share this lifestyle with you by carefully curating kits with hardy plants that will ease your anxiety about greenery care. We have thoughtfully designed our subscription service as a program that will take you through different levels of plant care. We'll provide you with all the tools, tips, and hardy plants. Whether you are a plant newbie or an aesthete who wants to acquire some tasteful new planting accessories— we can hook you up!

—PUNEET SABHARWAL AND BRYANA SORTINO

BROOKLYN
PLANTOLOGY

SERVING LUSH
LEWKS GALORE
:camera: @brooklynplantology

Dahling, who doesn't love a plant shop serving lush lewks for days!?! I found the botanical beauty that is Brooklyn Plantology during one of my summer Brooklyn biking treks. I had heard about the shop through a friend, who described the spot as a "warehouse of greenery." Gurl, you know she had to check this place out once I heard those words.

BROOKLYN PLANTOLOGY, formally known as Lawrence J. Lapide, Inc., was established in 1946 in the Brooklyn Terminal Market, originally as a small family-owned business predominantly selling seedless watermelon—it was one of the first of its time. As the company expanded, the team began buying up the out-of-business stores located next to it, and soon came to own over 20,000 square feet of space. This allowed them to sell more than just watermelons, and they added plants, garden tools, and seasonal decor to dress up your green gurls. With a wide variety of green gurls, this shop is considered the largest plant retail company of its kind in the New York City and tristate areas.

I've always enjoyed my trips to this fabulously large shop because space in NYC is usually limited and it's refreshing to just be in a large space with a bunch of greenery that you can take home with you.

SOME LUSH TAKEAWAYS

→ Get to know the history and story of how your local plant shops came to be! It puts thangs into perspective and makes you fall in love with their lushness even more!

→ Don't be afraid to venture outside of your neighborhood when searching for those new lush spots to shop! This shop was a lil trek from my apartment, but it was worth the trip and now I visit regularly!

Our plants come from all over the world. This enables us to give you the most colorful, exotic, and beautiful plants on the planet. Since we deal with so many suppliers, we can also give you the lowest prices anywhere. We have annual and perennial varieties that you can get to decorate and beautify your yard, home, office, or business. From cacti (succulents) to evergreens and tropical plants, we will always have something you want.

—BROOKLYN PLANTOLOGY TEAM

CHAPTER 6

THE LOVE IS IN THE DEETS
Planters and Soil Mixtures

Dahling, as much as I love to go plant shopping (and gurl, she LOVES plant shopping), the whole fabulous experience would not be complete without pairing my green gurls with their own lil planters!

PLANTERS PROVIDE OUR LUSH KWEENS with the space to spread their roots, anchoring themselves into that fresh soil and growing into their green glory. It's their home within a home, hunty, and it's a crucial ingredient as you create and build your plant care recipe for each of your green gurls. When out and about in your local plant shops and nurseries, you'll find that a majority, if not all, of those lush green gurls are in plastic containers, aka their nursery pots. These are the vessels that plants are either grown or placed in for distribution to make it to those plant shop shelves. Most of the time our green gurls are jam-packed into these lil vessels, which are really meant to be temporary homes. They need space to spread their roots, so my general rule whenever I welcome a new green gurl into my home is to pair her with a new planter that is about 2 inches larger than the nursery pot. It is a common myth that bigger is better when it comes to picking a planter for your green gurl, dahling.

MOST HOUSE PLANTS prefer thangs to be a bit snuggier, as their roots tend to take their time as they expand and grow rather slowly. If a green gurl is placed in too large of a planter, her roots will be surrounded by soil that she is unable to reach, which means she will not be able to pull water from that soil fast enough. This will result in the soil staying wet for too long, drowning the roots and causing root rot. Providing that kween with just the right amount of room to grow, but not too much room, ensures that her roots will reach all parts of the soil, which means the soil will dry out quicker and oxygen can reach the roots—this is a must! In the botanical scene, you will find that most pots fit into a size system that increases by twos: 2 inches, 4 inches, 6 inches, 8 inches, and so on. So, if your green gurl has a nursery pot that is 4 inches wide, then you'll want to go with a 6-inch planter for that particular kween.

While picking a planter is simple and effortless for me now, when I was a plant parent newbie, this process seemed like a daunting task. With numerous kinds of planters, pots, and vessels to choose from, how could I possibly choose the right lil mini homes for my green gurls as I welcomed them into my life? And so I experimented, as I often do with my plants, trying different kinds of planters made from various materials over the years. Taking note of how their lil vessels impacted their lush growth, the soil moisture throughout the seasons, and my overall care routine taught me a few thangs about the kind of plant nurturer I am and which planters werk best for me as I care for my ever-growing plant fam.

So let's dive into some of my fav planters, some thangs to keep in mind when selecting which ones may werk best for you and your green gurls, and then we'll get down and dirty as we talk through making your own soil mixture recipes!

TERRA-COTTA PLANTERS

GURL, SHE LOVES a classic, and unglazed terra-cotta pots are just that! The material, terra-cotta, is a natural clay that is fired at over 1,000°F (538°C). The iron compounds in the clay give terra-cotta that fabulously warm color that I love and adore, a shade between orange and brown, a rusty, muddy hue. When the clay is fired, minerals are melted and moisture is released, resulting in a fierce hardened and porous material. I love terra-cotta pots for several reasons:

1   They are quite easy to find at your local plant shops and nurseries and inexpensive compared with other planters and pots out there.
2   The porous nature of this earth-based material allows for air and moisture to pass through the walls of the pot; this can be helpful in preventing over-watering and eventual root rot. As a plant parent who has a history of over-watering her green gurls, this is helpful! Note: You may notice a white substance growing on these pots. This is simply calcium and other minerals found in our water or in fertilizers left behind when the water dries up. While this will not be of immediate harm to your green gurl, I often wipe it off with a mixture of white vinegar, rubbing alcohol, and water.
3   They are breakable! Now, this may not seem like a pro, but if you ever find your green gurl stuck in her planter when it's time to repot her, then you may think differently, hunty! I take a hammer to any terra-cotta pots I can't get my kweens out of when repotting them. Tugging on that green gurl too hard could damage her root system. I'd rather break apart an inexpensive pot than risk damaging the foundation of my green little kween.

PLASTIC PLANTERS

DAHLING, I HAVE A limited relationship with plastic, as it is something I am trying to use less of in my daily life, but I have found it to be useful in caring for a few of my green gurls.

1   I like to repurpose the nursery pots that my green gurls come in, holding on to them so that I can use them later. She's a kween on a budget, so making use of all those nursery pots of various sizes is a cute economical choice. I measure the pots out and just select one that is 2 inches larger than the original nursery pot that the kween came with. Coins saved!

2   Plastic pots are not porous, so they retain moisture and water well. This is a fab situation for our green gurls who prefer more moist soil. I tend to keep ferns or freshly propagated cuttings I've potted in fresh soil in plastic pots, as I sometimes struggle with keeping their soil how they like it, dampened and moist. Now, if you are a kween who struggles with being an under-watering plant parent, then utilizing plastic pots may be the route to go. In plastic pots your green gurls can go longer periods without a drank.

3   Plastic pots don't break easily, are lightweight, and are less likely to shatter should your green gurl have a tumble. While it is just me and my green gurls in my lil Brooklyn apartment, I know that some folks have little humans and furry frands that they care for! Using plastic pots may be a safer option for those folks who have curious little minds wandering their space looking to explore the lil indoor jungle before their eyes.

FIBERGLASS PLANTERS

THIS KWEEN LOVES a cute botanical aesthetic and lives for decor, so I dib and dabble in fiberglass planters occasionally when I want a pop of color or unique shapes on my plant shelves.

1   Made from composite materials formed from fibers of spun glass that are held together with resin, these planters can come in a variety of colors and shapes. My green gurls are living, breathing werks of art and sometimes I enjoy dressing them up in a planter that is serving that artsy vibe. The material can also be made to mimic a bunch of different materials: wood, terra-cotta, cement, stone, or ceramic. It can be glazed, slick and modern chic, or even aged to serve that vintage lewk! When it comes to decorating, the possibilities with this material are endless. This also means that these planters tend to be a bit pricier, so I try to save up some coins before investing in this kind of vessel.

2   This material is not porous, so it retains moisture and water well for any of those green gurls that prefer soil more dampened than dry. I tend to keep ferns, begonias, and other tropical kweens in these kinds of pots. The material also makes them quite sturdy and durable for outdoor use, gurl. So, if you have an outdoor garden, these planters could be a cute situation for you and your green gurls.

3   These planters are impressively lightweight, and for my larger green gurls this is a saving grace! Larger plants = larger planters = a heavy situation. The first time I held a fiberglass planter I was shook at how light it was. My very first fiberglass planter was about 12 inches and I held it up with one finger; from that moment on I knew that these planters would be for my larger green gurls.

DRAINAGE HOLE: TO HAVE OR NOT TO HAVE?!

BEFORE MAKING YOUR final decision on the planter you'll eventually pair with your green gurl, flip that planter upside down to see if there is a drainage hole at the bottom. Drainage holes are extremely helpful during the watering of your plant fam, as they allow any excess water to drain from the pots. When watering your plants, you want to make sure to water the soil evenly and thoroughly, and a key sign that you have done just that is water falling from the drainage hole. It can be helpful to bring your green gurls to the sink or bathtub to let that water fall from the drainage hole. Or you can purchase lil saucers to catch the water. The drainage hole also ensures that there is no stagnant water left at the bottom of the pot, which could lead to over-watering and root rot. Of my 200+ green gurls, I only have four in planters without a drainage hole. With my tendency to over-water, my life is so much easier if I don't have to guesstimate how much water is just enough. I pour the water into the pot and the excess water drains out, leaving my green gurl thirst-quenched. It's a cute and easy process. I often call the water dripping out of the drainage hole tears of joy, simply because I imagine my green gurls being thankful for the drank and crying tears of joy as a result. This process werks for me, but it may not suit all the plant parents out there, dahling.

I have plant frands who prefer and enjoy planters without drainage, and have a better knack than I'll ever have for knowing how much water is just right for their green gurls. Most of these plant frands are plant parents of the under-watering variety, so it makes sense that they would prefer these kinds of planters.

If you decide to go with a planter without drainage, be sure to put a layer of pebbles, aeration stones, or lava rocks at the bottom of the planter. This allows for the excess water to flow into the space with the pebbles, away from the soil and the roots of your green gurls. This lil method reduces the chances of your green gurl experiencing root rot. I've also seen folks drill drainage holes into pots that didn't have one. Fiberglass planters are typically more decorative than functional, so I've also used them to house some of the kweens I have in bland plastic pots to add some pizzazz to those kweens' lewk. There are ways to werk around the lack of a drainage hole, dahling.

Overall, if you are a plant parent newbie, I encourage you to seek out planters with drainage holes. It will make your life a lot easier not having to guesstimate how much water is just right, and it will help keep your green gurls lewking lush.

LET'S TALK ABOUT POTTING SOIL, HUNTY!

KWEEN, LET'S GET those hands dirty, cuz potting soil is the next thang on the list as you prep to welcome your new green gurl into her new planter! This medium provides our green gurls with a foundation in which their roots can expand and holds the nutrients needed for these kweens to grow. The potting soil often used for indoor house plants is a mixture of a bunch of different materials like sphagnum peat moss, bark, perlite, vermiculite, compost, sand, wood fiber, and/or coconut fiber designed for plants that live in containers or planters. And gurl, this mixture is actually soilless! Yas, kween, most potting "soil" does not actually have topsoil in it! Topsoil is the natural layer of soil we see when we step outdoors and into our parks, forests, jungles, and savannahs, having formed at the surface of our precious planet over millions of years from rock decomposition and wind and water movement.

While topsoil mixtures are used in outdoor gardening, topsoil is far too dense for our potted kweens. Topsoil can also carry fungus and other planty pathogens that can be harmful for our green gurls. Potting soil is sterilized, and thus safer for potted plants, and has a loose and fluffy texture that allows for proper aeration, drainage, and root growth. Some potting soil contains added fertilizers, a mixture of minerals that are essentially vitamins for our green gurls, their roots absorbing all those delicious nutrients when the water releases them in the soil mix. Other potting soil mixes may not have fertilizer added, so be sure to take note and read the ingredients for the one you choose.

When brainstorming your potting soil mixture recipe, make sure it is tailored for your particular green gurl. Cacti and succulents prefer a coarse and sandy mix; ferns enjoy a mix with more peat moss or sphagnum for moisture retention; seedlings + rooting cuttings like a lighter and finer-textured mix; most tropical kweens enjoy a balanced, well-drained, and aerated mix, while many orchids thrive in just fir bark or sphagnum moss. Now, while you are able to find these specific blends already packaged and ready for purchase at most of your local plant shops and nurseries, it can also be fun to add various ingredients to an all-purpose potting soil mixture to make your own DIY soil blend. I find it to be a therapeutic process, gurl, and it's the perfect excuse to get your hands dirty! Here are some of the ingredients I add and mix into all-purpose potting soil when brewing up my own blends for my green little kweens.

COMPOST

Made up of a variety of organic substances, such as plant and animal matter, and containing a bunch of fabulous beneficial microbes, compost retains moisture, increases soil organic matter, and provides a slow release of nutrients important for that new growth, dahling. Over time, most potting soil becomes depleted of nutrients, and mixing compost into the top few layers of that soil is a wonderful way to give your kweens a nutritional boost! How much compost depends on the size of the plant and the pot; too little will not provide enough nutrients and too much could be harmful for your green gurl. I stick to between half an inch to an inch of compost in the top layers of the potting mix, depending on the size of the planter.

SPHAGNUM PEAT MOSS

The primary and base ingredient in most potting soils is sphagnum peat moss. This is not to be confused with sphagnum moss, which is made up of long, fibrous strands of plant material, dahling. Sphagnum peat moss is a dark brown fibrous material that forms when sphagnum moss and other organic materials decompose in peat bogs over thousands of years. This material is fabulous for absorbing + retaining moisture, and acts as a medium that holds any added nutrients so that they aren't rinsed out when we water our green gurls. I tend to add a lil more of this ingredient to any potting mix for plants that prefer more moist and dampened soil.

SAND

Made from crushed granite, quartz, or sandstone, horticultural sand improves the drainage of any soil when added. I use this in the soil blends of cacti and succulents, who enjoy their soil drying out completely in between waterings.

FIR BARK

Made from the ground bark of fir trees, these bits of chopped wood lighten up the potting mix by increasing the porousness of the soil, allowing air and water to travel freely in the mix. I tend to add fir bark into the potting soil of green gurls that prefer not to sit in damp or moist soil for too long. These bits of wood can help to make sure that soil dries out in a timely fashion and reduce the chances of over-watering.

PERLITE

Ever notice those lil white faux-Styrofoam balls in potting soil? Well, they have a name, dahling: perlite. A mined and volcanic glass, when crushed and heated, perlite expands, making those lightweight particles placed in potting soil to increase pore space and improve drainage. While a majority of potting soil already has bits and pieces of perlite in the mix, I add a bit more for any green gurls that enjoy well-drained, aerated soil.

WHEN PURCHASING or brewing up your own blend of potting soil, a great general rule of thumb is to make sure the mix is not dense. It should be light and have pore space for air, water, and those roots to flow through with ease. After months and months of watering our kweens in their lil planters, without those fierce earthworms and tiny critters that aerate the soil in their natural habitat, the soil can become compacted, which is a tragic situation for those roots. Materials like perlite, fir bark, and sand can help prevent this compacting. I also sometimes take a chopstick and poke holes in my green gurls' soil to make lil pathways for air and water to flow through.

Moral of this chapter, dahling: Pairing your green gurl with a planter she'll enjoy and a potting soil blend that she can sink her roots into with ease will set her up to thrive ever so beautifully in your space.

CHAPTER 7

THAT PLANT PARENT PATIENCE

Gurl, growth takes time! As you welcome your green gurls into your home, be patient with these kweens as they get adjusted to their new environment. They are getting used to new lighting conditions, room temperatures, and humidity levels, so it is only natural for them to experience stress when you welcome them to a new home.

ONE SUMMER I FELT BOLD and decided to welcome Ms. Fiddle-Leaf Fig (aka Ms. *Ficus lyrata*) into my plant fam. This green gurl had been on my plant wish list for a couple of months and I was simply obsessed with her chic, heavily veined, violin-shaped leaves. I had done all my research! This tropical kween is native to western Africa and grows naturally in lowland rainforest environments. I had read that in the wild this green gurl can grow up to 40 or 50 feet tall, with leaves as long as 18 inches and 12 inches wide. I had already picked out a spot where she would get a lot of indirect, ambient light, and a dabble of direct sun throughout the day. I found that the general consensus regarding watering was that this kween enjoys thorough waterings, but does not like to sit in water. So I would place her roots in well-drained soil and let the soil dry out completely before giving her another drank. As for humidity, these green gurls are native to tropical rainforests and thrive in warm, humid environments, so I knew that my humidifier would come in handy. I had heard that she could be a temperamental kween, but I felt ready to take on the challenge; after all, this kween of a plant parent did all her research and was prepared!

I brought Ms. Fiddle-Leaf into her new home and repotted her later that day. Figured that it would be best to get her acclimated to her new planter as quickly as possible, so she could get comfy and settled in the bright little corner of my bedroom I had picked out just for her. Gurl, I was checking in on this kween every day, making sure she wasn't dropping any leaves, that no leaves were beginning to brown, checking her soil to see if it had become too dry. I was one of those helicopter plant parents! I was hoping that I would see some new growth, but nothing was happening. She had been in her ideal sunny lil corner for about two weeks and no new growth. *If she is not growing during the growing season, then I must be doing something wrong,* I thought.

I figured that perhaps the spot I had placed her in was not bright enough and so I began to move her around my room, trying to see if brighter spots would provoke her to start serving new growth realness. After moving her around a few times, there came a morning when I found one of her leaves on my bedroom floor. Gurl, I was devastated! I had been so attentive, putting in all this time and energy and she lost a leaf! That kween eventually went to the lil botanical garden in the sky. I tried a number of times to care for this kween only to end in a classic plant-parent fail each time. I came to the conclusions that: 1) I was not as good a plant parent as I thought, and 2) Ms. Moody Fiddle-Leaf Fig and I were not a match.

Two years later I decided to give caring for Ms. Fiddle-Leaf Fig another try. I remember the moment so vividly. I was in a coffee shop on a random weekend werking on some planty projects; it was a cute day and she was feeling productive. I was in such a groove that I was a bit startled when I heard a voice say, "Oh, you're into plants too?!" There was a woman sitting next to me with her laptop open werking on her own projects. She had glanced over at my laptop filled with images of greenery I was using to create a planty workshop slide deck.

"Yeah, I'm pretty obsessed with them!"

She had a plant fam of her own but was moving to Cali later that week and had decided to leave them with her roommates. "Moving is stressful, and I don't want to put my plants through that," she said with such calmness in her voice that you knew that she had thought long and hard about that decision and made her peace with it. As plant parents do, we went through our green gurl lists, sharing the occasional photo we had snapped on our phones. She showed me an image of a 7-foot fiddle-leaf fig in her gorgeous, classic prewar living room, and, gurl, I gagged! "How in the world are you able to keep that kween thriving and like she is?!" I was shook, reminded of my own struggles with that kween. She looked at me and said just one word, "Patience."

I looked at her, intrigued by her answer. She went on to tell me that she hadn't moved that kween from her spot in over four years. "She struggled at first when I brought her home, but after a month or two she had acclimated, and was thriving." Our conversation was cut short as her wife arrived, ready to get back to packing. We said our friendly goodbyes, and I sat with her story. We exchanged pronouns, but I can't recall catching her name, and I wish I had because that conversation grounded me in so many ways.

Perhaps that is what I did wrong. I didn't give Ms. Fiddle-Leaf Fig a chance to get settled. I needed to leave her be and let her get acclimated to my space on her own schedule, not mine. I left the coffee shop shortly after and headed to a plant shop to pick up my tenth fiddle-leaf fig. Happy to say that with some TLC and patience this green gurl is thriving and serving lushness. We just have to be a bit more patient with some plants, as they may need a little more time to get settled into a new space.

IT TOOK ME A WHILE, but I've had to learn to practice that plant parent patience! Let's say it again for the folks in the back: PRACTICE PLANT PARENT PATIENCE! It is our role as the proud caregivers of these green kweens to minimize the stress they may experience when we welcome them into our spaces, and this can be done in a multitude of ways, dahling:

1   **You do not have to repot them into their new planter right away.** Nowadays I tend to wait at least a week or two before repotting any new green gurl I bring into my home. This allows for her to hopefully experience any stress in waves, rather than all at once. If the plant is not bursting out of her nursery pot, I let her sit in her plastic planter getting adjusted to the light, temperature, and humidity levels in my space first. If she seems steady after a week or two, then I'll repot her with some fresh soil in her new planter. The roots may experience some stress, but at least she is somewhat settled into her new surroundings.

2   **Leave that kween in one spot.** My biggest mistake with Ms. Fiddle-Leaf Fig was moving her all about in my space the first few weeks. By moving her all around, I robbed her of a chance to get settled into her own daily routine. In that original spot I had placed her in, perhaps she was becoming used to the cool morning breeze that flew through that corner. Perhaps she had begun to expect and look forward to that hour of direct afternoon sun that hit that corner around 2 PM. Perhaps she enjoyed cooling down in the evening from the mist of my humidifier that I had placed in that same corner and would turn on after a long day of werk. Instead I moved her about so much that she was in a constant state of newness, unable to really adjust to a particular spot in my space. So, I've learned to leave any new green gurls in one spot for at least a month before deciding to move them to a new location in my space. Give that kween time to adjust and trust that you have chosen the best spot for her.

3   **Your green gurls may experience shock, and that's okay.** We all know that moving is stressful, and the same goes for our green gurls! When being welcomed into a new environment, they may experience shock. Shock could look like leaves drooping or a leaf or two falling from the stem, vine, or base of the plant. In most situations this shock is a temporary experience for your new green gurl; as she gets adjusted to her new home, she'll bounce back. We just have to give our kweens time to bounce back! There are generally two kinds of shock:

PLANT SHOCK: This is a generalized term naming the stress a plant may experience due to abrupt changes in its overall situation: temperature changes, a different watering schedule, overfertilizing, changes in lighting, and/or drastic changes in humidity levels.

TRANSPLANT SHOCK: This is the stress that our green gurls experience when they are uprooted and/or repotted from their nursery pot to a new planter.

4　**Don't be all up on your green gurls; give them room to breathe.** It's cute and necessary to occasionally check in on that new green gurl, but don't be a helicopter plant parent like I was with Ms. Fiddle-Leaf Fig back in the day. Check in on that kween occasionally and give her the time she deserves to bounce back from any shock she may be werking through.

5　**No new growth, no problem!** In a state of shock your green gurl may be conserving and concentrating her energy on maintaining what she has. That plant may not be in a state to serve new growth realness just yet, and that is okay. Also, some plants are just slow growers and take their well-deserved time before putting out new leaves. I've also had experiences where I have brought plants home that were serving new growth realness with cute baby leaves, only to have those baby leaves not make it. Shock signals an interruption in the systemwide cycle performed by the roots and the leaves. Transpiration (the evaporation of moisture from the leaves) activates the movement of water and nutrients through the roots. Through photosynthesis, this intake of water and nutrients is converted into energy and food for this kween to sustain herself. This process is disturbed as we move her around and introduce her to new soil, which can cause younger, more vulnerable leaves to fall off. My green gurls are a constant reminder that growth is a process that takes time, patience, and energy! As you bring that lush greenery into your space, understand that those green gurls deserve the opportunity to get a grasp on their new surroundings and they'll be serving that new growth realness when they are well and ready!

There is a beautiful and intricate stillness that comes with growing plants, and you deserve to enjoy every minuscule moment of it. Don't rush it, and understand that all of this is simply a part of the journey of being a plant parent. I've come to understand that just as I have my flow and rhythms through the day, my green gurls need to be able to establish their own flow and rhythms as well. By practicing that plant parent patience, I have been able to slow down, take in the nature around me, and just enjoy the process of bringing greenery into my space. It has also allowed me to manage any stress or anxiety that may come with welcoming a new green gurl into my home. Will this green gurl get adjusted? Did I pick the right spot? Will she drop a leaf today? No longer do I flood my mind with numerous anxiety-provoking plant parent questions, hunty! It takes away from the joy! I put trust into my research and decisions about the green gurls I bring into my home and I trust in the resiliency of those green gurls to be able to get settled just fine with a lil bit of tender loving care and time.

AND, because I know that practicing patience is easier said than done, here is a lil meditative exercise I tend to immerse myself in when I begin to lean into my impatient tendencies . . . a lil somethang somethang that helps me slow down and calm my bawdy, mind, and spirit.

> "My green gurls are a constant reminder that growth is a process that takes time, patience, and energy!"

ACTIVITY

BREATHE, GURL

Find Mother Nature; she's all around you. To begin, find a spot in your space or outside where Mother Nature can be with you. If you have a place you go to mentally or physically that allows you to be with nature, whether it's the tree in your backyard, that green gurl on your office desk, or the grass between your toes in your favorite park . . . give yourself a lil shimmy, then let your energy be calmed by the presence of that gorgeous greenery right next to you, and breathe.

inhale . . . exhale . . . inhale . . . exhale

Get comfy, gurl. Wherever you find yourself, sit that fabulous bawdy in a comfortable position with your feet flat on the ground and your back in an upright position. Let those hands rest wherever they're comfortable. Unclench that jaw, dahling, and just be. Soften your gaze as you read these words. Shift your attention from the outside world to inside yourself, and breathe.

inhale . . . exhale . . . inhale . . . exhale

Tune in to that bawdy. How does your bawdy feel, gurl? From the tips of your toes to the top of your forehead, take your time to check in and reconnect to your physical presence. As you move your attention up your bawdy, take note of any tension or pain points, the texture of your clothing against your skin, the temperature of the environment. What are the places on your fierce and beautiful bawdy that feel most vibrant or dynamic? Lean into that vibrancy—you are resilient, magical, and beautiful. Relax any areas of tightness or tension, and breathe.

inhale . . . exhale . . . inhale . . . exhale

Tune in to your breath. Breathe in and breathe out, dahling. Notice the different sensations that come with each inhale and exhale. Cool air enters and warm air exits. Focus on your breath, and if you find your mind wandering, it's okay gurl . . . just focus on finding your own natural flow and rhythm of your breath. Feel your breath in your bawdy, in your abdomen, your chest, your throat, your nostrils. Let the air fill your bawdy, hunty. Sit with the stillness of this moment.

Take in that greenery. Notice the lushness around you. A tree, a shelf filled with plants, a bouquet of flowers, a dandelion growing through the concrete: Mother Nature is serving viridescent vibes all around you. Take the time to soak up that lushness and appreciate that natural, resilient beauty. Do you notice any new growth? Take a mental note of those fine details of the leaves that you may have not noticed before. What color are the leaves? What texture is that green gurl serving? What direction is she growing? Appreciate that foliage in all her beauty, and breathe.

inhale . . . exhale . . . inhale . . . exhale

Bring it back to the bawdy. When it feels right, come back to your mind, bawdy, and spirit. One more INHALE . . . one more EXHALE and let that bawdy sink into a deep relaxation before you bring yourself back to the present moment. Thank yourself, gurl. You created space for yourself to just be, and you deserved every second of it.

CHAPTER 8

BUILDING YOUR LUSH ROUTINE

When I tell folks that I have over 200 green gurls in my lil Brooklyn apartment, my words are often met with a reaction of utter surprise that I have managed to build such a lil indoor oasis. Inevitably, this shock is followed by the question "What does a care routine for 200+ plants look like?"

I ALWAYS HAVE FUN ANSWERING, as it is an opportunity to verbally reflect on a process that has changed, grown, and evolved over these past five years of this lush journey; my plant care routine is something that I have and will continue to build and work at over time as I grow as a plant parent.

Dahling, my plant care routine is a daily activity that I find great joy and happiness in. It is a space that allows me to interact with the intricate beauty of nature in the cozy comfort of my own home. It's an opportunity to whisk myself away from the hecticness of everyday adulting. It's an activity of solitude that has given me moments to be introspective and reflective about how I am caring for myself. It's something that I have made fun for myself and have integrated into my everyday. My plant care routine is something I can simply not imagine being without, because it is a form of self-care for my mind, bawdy, and spirit. It replenishes me.

"I incorporated my plant care routine into my everyday instead of treating it like one big tedious chore."

NOW, THIS WAS NOT always the case! There were moments when this kween was a plant parent newbie and my planty routine was more of a chore. It was something that I tried to bunch up into one day, rush through, and get done. I had yet to find joy in the process of caring for my green little kweens. Gurl, this led to many plant parent fails and my green gurls serving less than lush lewks!

It was the second summer of my being a plant parent when I began to realize that I had to make some changes to how I was caring for my plant fam. The summer prior I had bought my first plant, Ms. Marble Queen pothos, and I had spent the fall and winter slowly growing my group of green gurls. As spring approached, I had about twenty-five green little kweens in my lil bedroom and I was excited that the growing season had arrived. I was ready for my room to be serving all kinds of botanical garden realness! My plant care routine at the time was a lil chore I rushed through on Sundays in 30 to 45 minutes. Rushing through this process led to some of my kweens experiencing root rot, due to over-watering. I was not taking the time to moisture-check their soil to see if they needed a drink of water. Some of my kweens were infested with pests, as I did not take the time to inspect the leaves to ensure that they continued to be pest-free or to see whether they needed pruning. I was not taking the time to really be with my green gurls, and they were suffering because of it.

My bedroom that summer was not serving the lush lewks I wanted it to, so I buckled down and really began to change how I incorporated my plant care routine into my everyday instead of treating it like one big tedious chore. And, gurl, now she has a growing list of planty routines. Here are some of my favs that will keep your green gurls lewking lush.

DESIGNATE A "WATERING DAY" AND CHECK THE SOIL BEFORE WATERING, DAHLING.

WATERING MY PLANTS is one of my favorite routines, and it's also one of the most important. Keeping my green gurls hydrated ensures that they stay looking lush, continue to grow, and keep on thriving. In the beginning of this journey, I sent a bunch of plants to that little botanical garden in the sky due to over-watering. Over-watering causes a plant to experience root rot, which destroys the plant's root system, which is not what we want, dahling. Mistakes provide an opportunity to learn and do better next time, and so I learned my lesson! A plant has a greater chance of surviving being under-watered than over-watered. So, this kween has had to learn to pay closer attention to the needs of her green gurls, allowing them to tell me what they need . . . and, hunty, they are a vocal bunch!

Most houseplants need to be watered only every 7 to 10 days in warmer months or every 14 days in colder months. However, watering schedules for each green gurl can vary based on the type of green gurl she is, the kind of pot you have her in, the soil mixture, even the weather that week, gurl (the amount of sunshine she got, the humidity levels, etc.). A common mistake is watering your green gurls lightly and frequently. This typically causes only the top layers of the soil to be saturated with water, leaving the roots below dry. The key is to designate a day for watering and soak thoroughly. Sunday is my watering day, and I water my kweens until I see water falling from the drainage holes of their planters, as this tells me that water has touched all the roots of my green gurls.

And while Sunday is this kween's official watering day, I've found that sometimes my green gurls are on different schedules. I try to give each of my green gurls the individual attention they deserve and so I always check their soil moisture every Sunday. I do

this by simply placing my finger 2 inches into the soil. A common mistake that I used to make was checking only the top layer of soil, and this led to many plant fails, hunty! If when I place my finger 2 inches into the soil, the soil is damp, then I leave that kween be, she's good; and if the soil is dry, then she's thirsty, and I give that kween a drink. For larger pots, I either use a moisture meter (a handy gadget to measure humidity in the soil) or I check the drainage hole to ensure that I'm knowing what's going on with the roots!

WIPE DOWN
THOSE LEAVES, GURL.

PLANT ARE NOT furniture, so they should not be collecting dust, dahling! Throughout the week I check in on my green gurls to make sure dust has not piled up on their leaves. These leaves are a plant's meal ticket, so removing any dust makes sure your green gurl catches as much sunlight as possible so she can do her thang—that good ole photosynthesis. A little damp cotton cloth with some cool water does the trick!

I have a rotating schedule, where I have specific green gurls that I check on each day during the morning or during an afternoon lunch break at home, or in the evening after the werk day is over. Dusting the leaves of 200+ plants in one go can seem a bit intimidating, but spreading the task through the week gives me small moments to escape and care for my green gurls.

GIVE YOUR GREEN GURLS
A SPRITZ, HUNTY.

EVERY MORNING, as I warm up my jasmine tea, I spritz some of my green gurls with water from a little misting bottle. It's relaxing, it's soothing, and my green gurls love it! The plants I spritz are epiphytes, those plants that grow on top of other plants or trees, coexisting in the most harmonious, harmless way. Some examples include the staghorn fern, green gurls from the *Monstera* family, mosses, orchids, and *Tillandsias*. In their natural habitat, these kweens derive their nutrients and other vitals from the air, water, dust, and debris around them.

Spritzing the aerial roots of these kweens, and in the case of my staghorn fern, spritzing the shield frond and her leaves, mimics the rainfall these kweens are used to and keeps them looking lush.

> **JUST A NOTE:** Not all plants need to be spritzed, as foliage that remains wet for an extended period is prone to the plant diseases, fungus, and mold that require a moist environment to grow. If you are hoping to provide your green gurls with a little humidity, then invest in a humidifier; your plants and your bawdy will thank you!

ROTATE THAT KWEEN.

HAVE YOU EVER noticed your green gurls growing toward light? Well, dahling, this is natural in the growing process that helps these kweens in the wild find that sunlight that keeps them thriving. As the sun travels across the sky throughout the day, windows tend to limit the amount of sunshine that our green girls get to enjoy, which sometimes leads to uneven growth patterns. Rotating your kweens will ensure they get an even amount of light, which will reduce your green gurl leaning toward the light source and may promote new growth in areas of her foliage that might otherwise be serving stagnate realness.

Rotating my green gurls is a routine that I do every month for some of my kweens and once every few months for others, it really depends on the green gurl and her growth patterns. My grandmother would rotate her plants a quarter turn every time she watered them, as an easy way for her to remember to make sure the sunlight was shining on them evenly. As a good general rule, if your green gurl is leaning toward the light or her leaves are lusher on the side with more sun exposure, then rotate that kween. We want to make sure she's a well-balanced kind of green gurl, dahling!

GIVE THAT GREEN GURL THE OCCASIONAL TRIM, KWEEN.

WHILE THE BEST time to prune your green girls is toward the beginning of the growing season, which is typically early spring for most of our green little kweens, there can be exceptions to this seasonal situation when it comes to removing dead leaves or stems. Year-round pruning can be quite helpful for our green gurls, as damaged or dead leaves, stems, and branches can be an energy drain for our kweens. By giving them a lil cut, we are taking some werk off their plate and letting them focus their energy on those lush healthy leaves + serving new growth realness! Trimming our kweens can assist them in serving fuller foliage chic when thangs get a lil leggy. Giving your kween the occasional trim can also be helpful in preventing those tragic plant pests from settling on her leaves, as pests tend to be attracted to decaying or dead leaves more than healthy ones.

I often prune my kweens during my morning routine, looking at the overall shape and structure of my green gurls' foliage. Are there any yellowing or brown leaves that I can spot? Are there any vines that look a lil leggy or leafless? Are there any leaves that have pests crawling on them? These are typically the quiet little questions going through my head during my daily morning check-in with my plant fam. Most yellowing and/or browning leaves should come off the stems with a lil tug, but if you find yourself needing shears to cut a thicker stem, be sure to sterilize them (I wipe my shears down with 70 to 100 percent isopropyl alcohol). Sterilizing your sheers prevents the spreading of any fungi, bacteria, or pests. And when I prune leggy vines that are pest-free, I tend to look for any nodes along the stem to see if propagation is possible. Nodes are small growth zones on our green gurls' stems and will often grow into a root system when submerged in water.

I used to dread seeing a yellow or browning leaf on my green gurls, but now I see it as an opportunity for new growth. We all need room to keep growing, and letting go of a decaying leaf or two is just what our green gurls need sometimes to be able to put energy into new thangs.

CHECK IN WITH YOUR GREEN GURLS; THEY'LL THANK YOU.

I CHECK IN ON MY green gurls every day. It's a soothing and relaxing routine that I have come to love. In particular, when there are moments where I'm anxious or feeling stressed, I'll take a pause and I'll just tend to my plants. And it gives me an opportunity to step away from technology, gives me an opportunity to rest my voice, gives me an opportunity to rest my mind and really just get back to the basics, having interactions with nature.

This routine is also fabulous for my green gurls because it provides me with an opportunity to check to see if there is any new growth, any leaves that need pruning, any pests on the leaves that I need to get rid of, if I need to rotate a kween to make sure she's not leaning too far toward the sun, or if perhaps it's time for a little repotting because she needs room to grow. Instead of taking one day to try to tend to all of these needs, I check on a few each day. It makes the experience of having 200+ plants to care for less overwhelming.

Dahling, I tend to sprinkle my plant routines throughout the week, giving me little nature breaks throughout the day. When I water my green gurls, I make it a party! I blast music, I put on a fun outfit, I pour myself a lil cocktail, and I tend to my plants. It's a whole entire mood, and it's so much fun! So ask yourself: How can you add a little pizzazz to your planty routines? How can you make them fun for you?

Caring for plants can be tedious and seem like a chore if you treat it that way! Build a plant family that vibes with you. There is no green thumb needed; you simply have to match the plants to the level of care you can provide. If you are a person on the go and may forget to water your plants, stick with cacti, succulents, and other desert plants. They don't need that much attention and actually thrive in neglect. If you are a person who loves to nurture, then you may

want to check out ferns and orchids, as both of these kweens need a bit of attention in order to thrive. Plants are like potential friends; you want to make sure you are both compatible. As you begin and continue to green up your life, you will create and build a green gurl care routine that werks for you.

PART 2

PLANT PARENTHOOD

HOW TO CARE FOR YOUR GREEN GURLS

CHAPTER 9

BUILDING YOUR GARDEN

Plant-Care on the Journey to Self-Care

When I welcomed my very first green gurl into my home, I knew I was beginning a new exploration of my own self-care, and, gurl, my mind, bawdy, and spirit were ready for a new journey!

PRIOR TO MY BEING A PLANT PARENT, I often relied only on community care to reenergize my heart and soul. She's a gregarious extrovert, so I often found my younger self relying on the presence of others to be energized, spiritually full. If there was an opportunity to be social, gurl, I was there and my spirit was happy, cuz those moments did and will always provide space for community building, friendships, connections, growth, love, dialogue, and the creation of beautiful memories with folks I love and cherish. But balance is key, dahling, and this kween did not have any. I subconsciously desired space to explore what it meant to truly enjoy my own company. To learn to create more moments for quality time with me, myself, and I. My journeying into plant parenthood was a manifestation of that desire.

AS I WALKED OVER to my local hardware store on that beautiful Brooklyn summer day, I thought of my grandmother. While she was a community-driven woman and loved being surrounded by the folks she loved, she also valued and created moments when she was the reason for her own happiness, when she was the author of her own joy. In the middle of her southwest Philadelphia neighborhood, she built herself a garden, a home, and raised a fierce family. Her time in her garden was sacred, and her trips and adventures to various community gardens, parks, and nurseries were hers. When my grandmother noticed my curiosity in this lush lil world she had built for herself, she welcomed me into it with open arms. She shared these moments with me as a child and showed me that this level of self-love and self-care was possible. I thanked my grandmother out loud as I walked down the street with my very first green gurl in my hands; I was about to begin a lush lil world of my own.

Throughout this leafy green journey, my green gurls have given me a pathway to carve out mental space to be reflective and introspective in how I care for my own mind, bawdy, and spirit. In my adventure of learning how to care for them and their beautiful intricacies, I began to dive into my own intricacies, learning how to better care for myself. There is a particular moment I recall when it had become clear to me that this botanical journey was one I needed to be enjoying and exploring— giving myself permission to be enveloped in this ancestral yet newfound passion. I was living with two roommates and thirty or so green gurls strategically placed in various nooks, corners, and shelves throughout the apartment. Lawd, bless my roommates' hearts for being so understanding of my growing botanical obsession! It was a Sunday and I had the apartment to myself for the day. It was watering day, dahling, and that meant that this kween was about to have a cute time with herself. As my plant fam grew, I had begun to block out Sundays for myself and my green gurls. I wanted to make sure I took my time in caring for my kweens. Those mornings would typically start with me playing a cute jazz café Spotify playlist and me fixing some jasmine tea to wake my bawdy up! Would hop in the shower, sing a tune or two, and get dressed in a cute lil comfy garment. She was about to spend the next two hours prancing around the apartment pruning, checking soil, watering, dusting leaves . . . she might as well serve a cute lewk doing it! My mother FaceTimed me just as Chaka Khan's "I'm Every Woman" was ending on my lil Sunday playlist and I had just wrapped up watering the green gurls in the common areas of the apartment.

She asked me what I was up to and I told her that I was having a party with my green gurls. She laughed and asked to see how some of the kweens were doing. I took my phone around the apartment and showed her my little potted bundles of joy. She then took her phone and proudly showed me her little green kweens. She had a fabulous outdoor garden just like her mother had, and a cute lil plant fam of her own. "Your great-grandmother was a gardener, your grandmother was one too, you know I love my garden, and now you're creating one for yourself. It feels nice, doesn't it?"

I remember her words so clearly, as if it were yesterday. We stayed on the phone through the afternoon talking about different care tips, plant parent struggles, our processes for caring for the nature we had welcomed into our homes.

I was beginning to be more intentional about putting that same love, attention, care, and patience (gurl, can't forget patience) into my own being, as I was putting into my green gurls, dahling! I was creating a garden where I began to be better and intentional about drinking water every day. A garden where I let my bawdy dance in the sunshine. A garden where I tended to the foundation upon which my roots anchored and expanded. A garden where I was able to put energy into my own growth. My mom had her garden, and she saw me building mine. She shined light on my garden that day when she named it, and I saw it clearly for the first time. And my mama was right, it felt so nice.

I wanted to share some personal mantras this plant parent journey has brought into my life, some daily reminders that have manifested through taking care of my green gurls. I've written these down for myself and will occasionally read over them . . . cuz some days you just need a lil refocusing.

1 Stay hydrated, gurl.
2 Let the sunshine in, hunty! Your body enjoys sunlight . . . it inspires the creative in you.
3 Healing and growth of your own heart, mind, body, and soul take time, love, energy, and intentionality. Give yourself grace and be patient with yourself, gurl.
4 While you are a kween who has worked hard at becoming good at taking care of herself (self-care), it is okay to lean into and seek support and tender loving care from friends and family (community care) . . . cuz sometimes you can't water yourself and that's okay.
5 We are all basically houseplants with complex emotions.

While my lil garden of personal growth has these mantras and a plethora of self-care options that I sprinkle throughout the days, weeks, and months, I've found that my mornings are often the moments when I am consistently engaging in care for my own spirit. Being a bit more patient and attuned to my own bawdy, I've come to realize that my morning is the foundation for the rest of my day. Dahling, her morning routine be meaningful and intentional! Been spending my early mornings slowly waking my bawdy and being: playing music that is soothing to my spirit, making up my bed, drawing back the curtain to let the light in, burning incense, drinking that delicious H_2O, spritzing the aerial roots of my green gurls, singing in the shower, FaceTiming my family and friends to say good morning as I fix a cute breakfast for myself, meditating and stretching my bawdy through a self-guided yoga sesh. There is such a stillness, a quiet, a calmness that comes with early mornings, that I've come to enjoy . . . so, gurl, she is using them wisely cuz that is what daily self-care looks like for me.

Gotta take care of that bawdy—exhaustion and burnout be real. So how can you better take care of your own emotional, mental, and physical well-being? How can you show up for yourself, so that you can show up for and build up others? This is a question I ask myself on the regular, as engaging in daily self-care is a lifelong learning process, and it looks different every day. Be patient with yourself, dahling, as you create, build, and explore your lush garden of self-care moments for you, yourself, and your own fabulous being.

And because we are basically houseplants with complex emotions, I want to share some of my own self-care routines that are integrally entwined with caring for my green gurls.

PLANT KWEEN'S Get 'That Bawdy & Spirit Movin' PLAYLIST

I'm Every Woman, CHAKA KHAN • Emotions, MARIAH CAREY • Dancing Queen, ABBA • Real Love, MARY J. BLIGE • Hey Mr. D.J., ZHANÉ • I Wanna Dance with Somebody (Who Loves Me), WHITNEY HOUSTON • Doo Wop (That Thing), LAURYN HILL • Water Me, LIZZO • Brown Skin Girl, BEYONCÉ, BLUE IVY, SAINT JHN, WIZKID • Appletree, ERYKAH BADU • Do It, CHLOE X HALLE • Golden, JILL SCOTT • What's Love Got to Do with It, TINA TURNER •

Respect, ARETHA FRANKLIN • I Will Survive, GLORIA GAYNOR • Ring My Bell, ANITA WARD • I'm Coming Out, DIANA ROSS • Where My Girls At, 702 • Square Biz, TEENA MARIE • My Lovin' (You're Never Gonna Get It), EN VOGUE • Got to Be Real, CHERYL LYNN • She Works Hard for the Money, DONNA SUMMER • Video, INDIA.ARIE • Soulmate, LIZZO • Mood 4 Eva (FEATURING OUMOU SANGARÉ), BEYONCÉ, JAY-Z, CHILDISH GAMBINO

LET THE MUSIC PLAY!

GURL, IF YOU DIDN'T KNOW already, this kween is all about playing a cute playlist and dancing to tha beat, with the trio that is me, myself, and I. Yas, she loves a lil dance-with-herself moment. As a person with bilateral hearing loss, I often don't catch lyrics, pitches, and certain sounds when I listen to a piece of music, but instead her bawdy is feeling the vibrations and catching the sounds and melodies she's able to, creating a new song that my senses have made just for me. I've also found that I attach songs to moments that become memories, rather than trying to focus on the lyrics. Most of the music I have on repeat is that nineties R&B. My dad played all those jams during my childhood, and sometimes she likes to revisit those childhood moments and emotions through music. Her relationship with music is a joyous and complex one, gurl.

She also be playing music for her green gurls, cuz she's that kind of plant parent, dahling. So naturally, a kween has to do a lil research on the effects of music on that green gurl growth. The research seems to point out that it isn't so much about the "sounds" of music, but more to do with the vibrations created by the sound waves. Simply put, the vibrations produce movement in those green gurls' cells, which stimulates the plants to produce more nutrients. Some studies have shown that our green gurls may prefer certain kinds of music based on the kinds of vibrations the sounds produce, and whether the pressure created is conducive to that kween's growth. Our green gurls have selective musical taste, dahling, and I ain't mad at it. And, gurl, because this planty research is multifaceted, some researchers don't believe it's the vibrations of the music but simply that a plant parent who plays music for their green gurls is most likely to be providing their plant fam with that top-level care and special attention, which is the ultimate root of those green gurls serving that lush new growth realness.

Either way, she's jamming away to some cute beats, enjoying the vibrations of the music, and she hopes her green gurls are too. And, dahling, as you tend to that beautiful garden of yours you may want a lil theme song or some background music to put a lil pep in your step. Hope you, your bawdy, and your spirit enjoy my playlist, dahling.

REST IS FUNDAMENTAL!

THIS KWEEN IS ALL about that good rejuvenation, relaxation, and rest! Sundays are my days for tending to my green gurls and resting my bawdy, cuz sometimes self-care is them midday naps, sleep, catnaps, a pause to close them eyes, gurl.

So, do our green gurls rest? She did a lil research, right before one of her catnaps. While our green gurls do not have a central nervous system, which regulates sleep for our bawdies, these kweens do tune themselves to a twenty-four-hour circadian rhythm, just like us. And when the sun goes down, dahling, these kweens do shut down certain processes, like photosynthesis, shifting the werk to delivering glucose (sugar, hunty) throughout the plant.

So you may wanna softly whisper "you betta werk" to your green gurls tonight.

Sometimes it can be difficult to rest—I've been there. So here is a lil exercise I tend to do to get my mind, bawdy, and spirit to wind down and prepare for rest.

ACTIVITY
4-7-8
BREATHING

BREATHING TECHNIQUES are helpful when you are trying to bring your bawdy to a state of deep relaxation, and this is one of them, kween. Developed by Dr. Andrew Weil, this lil exercise is designed to help focus on taking long, deep, rhythmic breaths in and out. I have found that it helps me unwind before bed after a long day.

Now depending on whether you are just trying to take a pause in the middle of the day or getting that bawdy ready for bed, you'll either want to find a place to sit comfortably or lie down to get started. Rest the tip of your tongue against the roof of your mouth (right behind your top front teeth) and keep it there throughout the exercise. You ready, dahling? Let's begin:

1

Let your lips fall apart and exhale through the mouth, empty your lungs of all that air and that anxious energy that is keeping your bawdy from being calm and relaxed.

2

Close those lips and slowly inhale through your nostrils, letting in that fresh air and that cool, calm, and collected energy your bawdy needs, as you count to four in your head.

3

Stay here with that air in your lungs and that energy in your being, holding your breath for seven seconds.

4

Exhale slowly from your mouth as you count to eight.

5

Inhale again, and you've started a new cycle of breath. Repeat this cycle for four full breaths, dahling, and enjoy that state of relaxation and calmness you so rightfully deserve.

PRODUCTIVITY AND PLANTS, PLEASE!

WHETHER I'M WERKING from my office or my home, my green gurls keep me in that productive mewd! Being creative and playful with greening up my office and my makeshift werk spaces has been the key to keeping thangs from getting a bit monotonous during the werk day. When a kween is werking from home, I move about my lil Brooklyn apartment trying out different spaces: the floor of my plant nook, my kitchen counter, on the couch in my living room, and even in my bedroom! This just keeps thangs interesting for me and gives me time to appreciate every square foot of my space—she pays that NYC rent, gurl, so she's gonna enjoy every inch of this apartment!

To jazz and green up each werk day, I've been choosing and placing a different green on my desk. I'll look at her leaves, check for new growth, see if she's due for a new pot, and basically spend the day appreciating her viridescent beauty. There are moments when a meeting may end a few minutes early, and for those five extra minutes I have until my next meeting I'll tend to my green gurls, refill the humidifier, or check to see if they need a drink of water. Sometimes I'll just peruse my green gurls, checking to see if there is any new growth or maybe I'll notice a fine detail that I hadn't seen before. Sometimes I'll just look upon my green gurls, I'll take a couple of intentional breaths in and out . . . and they've done it, my green gurls have reset me. Five minutes later I'm ready for my next meeting, replenished and ready to get to werk! Gurl, there is even research that shows that greenery in werk spaces has positive impacts on folks' well-being,

happiness, and productivity as compared to spaces without these kweens!

Each day I feel blessed to be able to create my own little happy green places in my office and my apartment that allow me space and vibes to get werk done while simultaneously getting to enjoy the botanical beauties that are my green gurls. Here are three of my fav green gurls that are fun for the space, cuz they spark a creative chord within this kween:

THE CROTON PETRA

"Now when it comes to sunlight, this kween will live her best life in a bright spot, as she needs lots and lots of light to keep her colorful foliage fabulous!"

SERVING BRIGHT AND colorful realness, Ms. Croton Petra, aka Ms. *Codiaeum variegatum* 'Petra,' is an evergreen shrub native to southern Asia and the western Pacific islands.

Now when it comes to sunlight, this kween will live her best life in a bright spot, as she needs lots and lots of light to keep her colorful foliage fabulous! Four to six hours of bright light is a cute situation for this kween. She can be a bit moody, as her colorful leaves may revert to shades of green if she is not getting enough light, while too much direct sun makes her leaves gray and dull. She's a tropical gurl and loves humidity, so make sure you have this kween in close proximity to a humidifier if you want her to live her best life! Let her well-drained soil dry out before watering her, and water her thoroughly and evenly when you do give her a drank! Pay attention to her leaves and she'll tell you if you are watering her too much or not enough; her leaves tend to droop or drop when the soil is too wet or dry.

Just like Ms. Fiddle-Leaf Fig, she does not like to be moved, so place her in one spot for 2 to 3 weeks before deciding to move her again. Let her figure out if she enjoys the spot you picked out for her! This kween's fave song must by "Toxic" by Britney Spears cuz she's moderately poisonous if ingested . . . so keep this kween away from children and pets.

2

THE FICUS AUDREY

SERVING #FICUSFRIDAY realness with her beautiful velvety and ovate leaves, Ms. Ficus Audrey, aka Ms. *Ficus benghalensis,* is a kween that I was absolutely obsessed with early on in my plant parent journey. You'll often find her in random restaurants or clothing stores going for a modern, minimalistic aesthetic. Some interesting thangs about this kween are that she's native to India, where she 1) thrives in massive proportions; 2) is among the largest trees in the world by canopy coverage, reaching 65 to 98 feet tall in her natural habitat; and 3) is the national tree of India.

This green gurl thrives in bright, indirect light; long periods of direct sunlight or low light are a no-no, hunty! The soil should be consistently and evenly moist, with small droughts in between waterings to allow the soil to dry out a bit. I have found that these kweens do better in plastic pots when in my care, as plastic pots retain moisture for longer periods of time and this ensures that the soil does not get too dry for too long. She's a tricky one because she's very sensitive to over-watering, but, dahling, her botanical beauty makes her worth the challenge!

Yellowing leaves at the bottom of her stem are a natural thang for her, as it's a part of her life cycle for older leaves at her base to yellow and drop. Brown edges on her foliage could mean a bunch of thangs, but are often a result of dry air, so crank up that humidity, dahling, if needed. And a sudden loss of younger leaves could be a sign of over-watering, so be sure to check the soil before watering this kween.

3 THE CHINESE MONEY PLANT

SERVING WELL-ROUNDED chic and circular realness, the Chinese money plant, aka Ms. *Pilea peperomioides*, is native to the Cang Mountain range in Yunnan Province of southern China, and was a kween that was difficult to come by in the States a few years ago, but in recent years has become an extremely popular kween, as this resilient and easy-to-care-for green gurl can be grown and propagated with ease.

I've found that my *Pileas* enjoy very bright indirect light (a filtered southern-facing window situation) and, gurl, they are responsive to that sunshine. These kweens tend to send all their leaves in one direction, trying to capture that sunlight, so I rotate them to ensure they remain well rounded. I try to stick to my regular watering routine for this kween, once a week during the warmer months and every 2 weeks during the colder months, making sure that her soil dries in between waterings. The well-drained soil I have her in (soil, perlite, and fir bark) ensures that I do not over-water this kween. And this green gurl is quite easy to propagate! The easiest way to do that is to take those lil baby kweens you see popping up from the soil. If the baby kween already has roots, place her into damp soil; and if she doesn't, you can place her in water and watch her roots grow, hunty.

CHAPTER 10

WATERING

H_2O: that delicious and foundational element for our green gurls' survival and growth, as for all life on earth. I remember when my elementary school science teacher taught her lesson on the importance of water on this precious planet. My young lil mind was so intrigued by the facts that water covers more than 70 percent of the surface of the planet and that when we are born into this world our bawdies are composed of 78 percent water—for plants this can be as much as 95 percent—this lil baby plant kween felt connected to nature more than ever.

LET'S GET OUR FEET WET and immerse ourselves fully into one of the most important plant care routines you'll dive into as a plant parent: watering your green gurls!

WATER: WHY SHE'S IMPORTANT

WATER PROVIDES OUR green gurls with that good ole structural support and serves as a vehicle to transport all those delicious nutrients and minerals throughout their stems and leaves. Think of plant cells like lil balloons. When they are filled with water, pressure within them, also known as turgor, helps the cells maintain their shape, keeping the cell walls at the right tension; in combination, all the cells support the plant's structure and keep her upright. When there is a lack of water, the cells become deflated, which leads to our green gurl serving wilted realness—she needs a drink in this situation, dahling. This liquid structural support allows our green gurls to adapt to their surroundings, flex their stems through the wind, and move their leaves toward the sun as it moves across the sky. This ensures that our green little kweens soak up as much sunshine as they can to photosynthesize.

When our green gurls are basking in the sunshine and photosynthesizing, water evaporates from the pores of the leaves. This process is called transpiration (their photosynthetic and respiratory process), dahling. The exhale of water vapor leaves room for the inhale of carbon dioxide from the atmosphere into the pores of the leaves. Carbon dioxide is essential for our green gurls to synthesize the sugars they use to feed themselves. As water evaporates from the leaves, this prompts our green gurls to soak up more water from the soil through their roots (bringing nutrients with it), helping to keep this self-sustaining internal system flowing and in balance. Our green girls have a beautiful rhythm with water, and our fabulous duty as plant parents is to ensure that we provide these green lil kweens with the occasional drink of that delicious H_2O so that they can keep serving lush lewks!

When it comes to the type of water I use to keep my green gurls hydrated, my go-to is tap water, as this is the most accessible and easiest option. And while tap water is just fine for a majority of our house plants (except air plants), there are other options to consider, dahling! So, let's go swimming in the sea of choices you have as a plant parent when it comes to different types of water for your lil indoor jungle and some of the pros and cons of each.

TAP WATER

FOR MOST FOLKS, including myself, tap water is a staple in daily household routines, including quenching the thirst of our green gurls. Turn on that faucet, and, dahling, you have an unlimited supply of the key element that keeps our green gurls lush. Depending on your location and how the water is fed to your home (a well on your property or your local water facility), the chemical and mineral content may vary. Tap water is often classified as "hard," high in dissolved minerals, or "soft," low in dissolved minerals.

PROS

→ Usually accessible, free, or at relatively low cost—and she is a kween on a budget.

→ Contains minerals like calcium and magnesium, which can be beneficial at certain levels for that lush growth, depending on the type of green gurl you are growing.

CONS

→ Often contains chlorine + fluoride, and this can be harmful for our green gurls at high levels.

→ When it evaporates, calcium and other minerals often build up in the soil, on the leaves themselves, or on the exterior of porous planters. With a simple mixture of water and lemon juice or vinegar, you can wipe down those leaves and those porous planters.

> **TIP:** To reduce the risk of your green gurls soaking up any harmful chemicals in your tap water, let the water sit out for about twenty-four hours before giving your plants a drink. This allows for some of the chemicals, like chlorine, to dissipate. Some plants are sensitive to chlorine compounds, including *Dracaenas*, ti plants, spider plants, prayer plants, *Calatheas*, and carnivorous plants.

BOTTLED/SPRING WATER

SPRING WATER is sourced from underground aquifers, which are basically large underground deposits of water, dahling. As the water naturally flows to the surface, it goes through Mother Nature's filtration process by traveling through bedrock—usually composed of limestone, which removes many impurities. It then is collected either at the surface spring or through a hole drilled into the source feeding the spring, then bottled for distribution.

PROS

→ May contain minerals that our green gurls enjoy, such as calcium or magnesium, depending on the source.

→ Contains little to no chlorine and/or fluoride, which our green gurls will appreciate.

CONS

→ It can get costly to buy bottled water, especially if your plant fam is a large one.

→ Plastic bottles are just not a mewd, and not very eco-friendly.

> **TIP:** The quality and mineral + chemical content of bottled water may vary depending on the source. Sometimes bottled water is simply tap water that has been enhanced in some way. Other sources include springs, wells, and surface waters. Do your research, dahling.

RAINWATER

THE ORIGINAL SOURCE of water for our green gurls in the wild, thriving in their natural habitats, rainwater can be a whole mewd, dahling.

PROS

→ The only coins you'll spend will be for collection containers.

→ Rainwater is naturally "soft" water, meaning that there are lower levels of minerals that can build up in the soil, on leaves, and on the surfaces of porous planters.

→ It is also free of chlorine and fluoride.

CONS

→ Depending on where you live, rainfall could be low, inconsistent, and hard to collect.

→ While rainwater is naturally slightly acidic because of the presence of dissolved carbonic acid, which is the same chemical that makes the bubbles found in soda pop (fun fact, right?!), water collected in areas near high manufacturing may be highly acidic due to that tragic pollution. And acid rain for our green gurls is just a big no-no, gurl.

TIP: The quality of the rainwater in your area may vary depending on where you are in the world. Do a lil research on the air quality and pollution sources where you live; it's just helpful to know these thangs in deciding whether you should be collecting rainwater.

AQUARIUM WATER

YAS, DAHLING, THAT murky water you pour out when cleaning that fish tank could be used as a cute lil cocktail of nutrients for your green gurls!

PROS

→ The nutrients that are often found in plant fertilizer accumulate in your aquarium. These include potassium, phosphorus, nitrogen, and beneficial bacteria.

→ It's always a cute sustainable situation when you can recycle used water in your home.

CONS

→ Water from very dirty aquariums that has not been changed for long periods of time may have too high a concentration of various chemicals, which could be harmful for our green gurls.

TIP: Water from salt-water aquariums should not be used for our green gurls, as the amount of salt could create a very toxic and harmful soil for our potted green gems. If you are using chemicals to adjust the pH level of the aquarium or to treat your fish, this water should not be used on any plants being grown for consumption and could be harmful for our houseplants.

TAP WATER HAS BEEN my go-to throughout my plant parent journey because it is most affordable, easily accessible, and works well for my green gurls. If I were living in an area where collecting rainwater was sustainable, then, dahling, she would be collecting rainwater. If I had an aquarium large enough to hold enough water for all 200+ of my green gurls, then she'd probably be recycling that fish tank water. Tap water works well for me now because of how life is set up for my green gurls and me in the current moment. As I continue to grow as a plant parent, and when the lush adventure of life takes me away from city living, I do plan to dip my toes in these other watery options for my lil indoor jungle. As you explore these various options, know that each has its pros and cons and that it is ultimately up to you to decide what is feasible, accessible, and sustainable as you care for your green gurls.

THE WATERING, DAHLING, THE WATERING!

NOW LET'S DIVE INTO the heart of this conversation, watering your green gurls! While it may seem like the simplest of tasks, it is a process that I hope you allow yourself the time, patience, and energy to navigate with intention. One of the most common reasons plant parents send their green gurls to that lil botanical garden in the sky is over-watering. This is because there are many variables that can make it tricky to know exactly when to water your green gurls, how often, and how much a particular green gurl may need to quench her thirst. Well, dahling, I gotchu! Through years of trial and error, practice, taking notes on my own plant parent watering fails, and an intentional dedication to do better for my green gurls, I've learned and will be outlining for you some thangs that will be helpful for you and your watering journey. Let's get into it, hunty!

STEP 1
SET A ROUTINE

I'VE SAID IT BEFORE and I'll say it again, dahling: Sunday is this kween's watering day. Having this weekly routine allows me to hold myself consistently accountable for taking time to pause and be with my green gurls no matter how hectic and busy my week has been. This routine also allows me to set a dedicated amount of time to care for my plant fam, ensuring that they get all the TLC they need to be healthy, fierce, and happy. Our green gurls enjoy when we are consistent with tending to them, as it becomes a part of their own natural rhythm and flow.

My watering routine typically starts during the morning hours, as it gives my kweens an opportunity to soak up as much water as they can before the sun begins to shine in full force through my southern-facing windows and begins to evaporate their drink of water. Watering in the morning hours was also helpful when my green gurls and I lived in spaces that didn't get a lot of natural light, as the multiple hours of daylight (even though the sunlight was minimal) helped to dry out the soil and ensure that my kweens were not sitting in wet soil for too long.

STEP 2
CHECK THAT SOIL

WHILE SUNDAY IS my official day with my green gurls, it does not mean that every kween will be getting a drink of water. Some of our plants are on different schedules and have different needs, dahling, so it is crucial that we give them the individualized attention they deserve by checking the soil moisture. For small to medium planters, I place my finger 2 to 3 inches into the soil. If the soil is damp, then I leave that kween be and will check in with her 2 to 3 days later to see if the soil has dried. When I am checking the soil and it's dry, then I'm giving that kween a drink . . . she's thirsty. For larger pots that are a little deeper, I tend to use a moisture meter, a houseplant soil probe (a lil gadget you can stick in the soil and collect lil samples of the soil below to test for moisture), or if I am able to lift the pot up, I'll check the dryness of the soil through the drainage hole. Tapping the topsoil of your green gurl is not enough; you want to make sure that you are touching the soil closest to the roots.

Do note, dahling, that different green gurls prefer different soil moisture conditions. Our cacti and succulent kweens prefer their soil to be kept on the dry side, as they are highly susceptible to rot if over-watered. Some tropical kweens like ferns, *Calatheas*, *Marantas*, and a variety of carnivorous plants enjoy their soil kept consistently moist. Many of the green gurls we welcome into our homes like the middle ground, preferring that their soil dry out a bit in between waterings.

STEP 3
SOAK THE SOIL EVENLY

GET THAT WATERING can ready, dahling, it's time to give your green gurls a drink! Room temperature water is best, as cold water can shock the roots, especially for our tropical kweens whose natural habitats are warm and humid. When watering my kweens I make sure to water evenly all the way around the pot, fully soaking the soil. This ensures that all the roots have been touched by water. When the water begins to trickle through the planter's drainage hole, these lil tears of joy signal to me that my green gurl is joyful and thankful for that drink of water.

If the soil is really dry, you may notice that the water runs through the pot quite quickly. This is simply because the soil has a difficult time absorbing the water during that first pour. Sometimes you'll even notice that the soil has dried up so much that a gap has opened up between its edge and the pot, which could cause the water to escape straight down the side, thus not fully soaking the soil and touching all the roots of your green gurl. If you find yourself in this situation, don't fret, dahling, just give that kween a second pour of water.

If you have a saucer at the bottom of the planter to catch any water that runs out, sometimes the soil will absorb back a bit more. Let that kween sit in that excess water for a couple of minutes just in case she wants more to drink, then be sure to dump out the rest, as we don't want our green gurls to be sitting in soggy soil.

If you have your green gurl in a planter with no drainage hole, then it is a game of guesstimating, dahling. Pour enough water onto the soil so that the excess water does not rise above the foundation of lava rocks, aeration stones, or other material you have resting at the bottom of that planter to prevent root rot. If you give your kween too much water, tip that pot on its side and allow that excess to drain out for a lil bit. You can also place a piece of cloth on the surface of the soil to let it absorb some of the extra.

TIP: Bottom watering is also a thang I tend to do at least once a month with my green gurls, as it is a fabulous way to give the roots near the bottom of the planter a good drink! Add water to the planter's saucer and let the planter sit in it, adding more water if she's thirsty and drinks up that first pour. The soil will soak up the water through the drainage hole, and will first touch the roots that often get the last bit of water when you water from the top. We want our green gurls' roots to be well balanced, dahling. Depending on the size of the planter, the amount of time you want to let that green gurl sit in that water will vary. For my green gurls in small- to medium-size pots, I let them sit for 10 to 15 minutes, checking just underneath the soil on the top to see if it is moist. For larger pots I let them sit for a lil longer, as there is more soil that needs to soak up that water—20 to 25 minutes usually werks perfectly. If there is any excess water after that kween has a drink, feel free to dump it out.

LET THE SOIL DRY OUT

YOUR GREEN GURLS have had their drink of that delicious water, and now it's time to leave your kweens alone to let them breathe and do what they do best: photosynthesize and serve lush lewks! Letting the soil dry out, even for our green gurls that enjoy more moist soil, is important for these kweens to remain healthy. The last thing we want our green gurls to experience is sitting in soggy soil for long periods of time. Plants use their roots to take in not only moisture, but also oxygen. If the soil is constantly wet, there will be little to no air pockets to allow the plant and her roots to breathe. This is what leads to root rot, and we ain't got time for that, dahling. Feel free to check in on your green gurls daily, but know that sticking to your watering routine is important and literally allows your green gurls room to breathe.

AS YOU ESTABLISH YOUR watering routine, take your time to make it a moment in the day that you look forward to! Enjoy this quality time with your green gurls. Eventually, you'll begin to get to know your green gurls a little better and will establish a flow and rhythm, a schedule with them. Be mindful that sometimes our watering routine has to change to meet the needs of our green gurls, as there are many factors that come into play when deciding whether our green gurls need a drink or not on that particular watering day you have set for yourself. During the warmer months I am watering most of my kweens weekly, as the high temperatures and longer days dry them out quicker. During the colder months I am watering my kweens less (every 2 to 3 weeks), as with colder temperatures and shorter days my green gurls are going dormant and not using as much energy, thus not needing as much water as they like to indulge in during the warmer months. The pot matters, hunty! Plastic pots retain moisture while terra cotta pots are porous, and this impacts how long the soil remains moist. Humidity impacts the soil moisture as well, kween. High humidity often leads to the soil staying moist for longer periods of time, and less humidity has the opposite effect. The very ingredients you use in your potting soil mix will also determine how fast it dries out. Take your time, embrace these variables, and get to know your green gurls' schedule. It's that individualized attention and TLC that will keep them thriving and healthy.

CHAPTER 11

PROPAGATION

Throughout this fabulous plant parent journey, I have accumulated a cute lil list of planty projects that I like to spend my weekends or downtime indulging in, cuz plant-care is a daily form of self-care for this kween. Sometimes thangs in life can get hectic and I find it necessary to have a lil list of thangs I can turn to when I need that opportunity to step away from technology, an opportunity to rest my voice and my mind and really just get back to the basics, having interactions with nature.

ONE PLANTY PROJECT I have come to enjoy quite a bit is plant propagation. Plant propagation is when you take a mature mother plant and either through cuttings, layering, or division you create a whole new green gurl to love, grow, and cherish! It is a fabulous way to expand your plant fam with the very green gurls you already love and adore, and it's a wonderfully thoughtful way to share that botanical love with the folks you cherish. I share my plants with my family and frands all the time, giving them cuttings of green gurls that have a special place in my heart. It's nice to know that the magic of the green gurls I have created moments and memories with is not contained within the walls of my apartment. She's all about sharing that botanical love, dahling!

"It was such a simple solution to ease some of my anxiety around the potential of losing green gurls that I have grown quite attached to."

THE FIRST GREEN GURL I ever attempted and successfully propagated was my Marble Queen pothos. It was about a year into my plant parent journey and a heartleaf philodendron that was a part of my original plant fam had left me for that lil botanical garden in the sky. It was my first plant loss, and this kween was devastated! I was that helicopter plant parent for the next couple of days, watching over my green gurls for the first sign of anything that wasn't serving healthy green lushness. The idea of having a green gurl that has grown with me, that I have created memories and moments with, being contained to just one planter had become a scary thought at the time after having just lost one of my precious kweens. A few days later I went on one of my usual plant perusing/planty retail therapy adventures through Brooklyn to get my botanical spirits up and came across three friends having a lil sidewalk sale. Their cute sidewalk setup was along my usual plant shop walking route and caught my eye because they had a few plants on their tables. Obvi, this kween was intrigued and skipped right on over to check out the greenery. They were all roommates and were moving to different states at the end of the month and had decided to sell a couple of thangs to get a few extra coins in their pockets.

There were some cacti, small succulents, a few pothos, and three baby *Philodendron cordatum* neons that looked like they were cuttings that were just potted in soil. Neon *Philodendron cordatum* is basically Ms. Heartleaf Philodendron, but instead of serving a darker lush green, she's giving neon green realness. I was intrigued and asked about the three mini kweens.

"Did y'all just pot these lil ones?" I asked, not sure which one of the three roommates they belonged to.

One of the roommates jumped up at the opportunity to talk plants; all the plants spread throughout the various tables were his. "Yup, the mother plant was struggling so I took some cuttings to preserve a few pieces, and voilà, saved the plant through these cuttings."

We talked for several minutes about his successes and fails with propagating different plants he had been growing. "It also makes traveling with plants so much easier. I'm not taking any potted plants with me, just cuttings, and I'm gonna grow my plant fam all over again."

I took one of the potted cuttings home with me that day and began to research plant propagation that evening. It was such a simple solution to ease some of my anxiety around the potential of losing

Ms. Heartleaf Philodendron
who inspired this propagating journey.

green gurls that I had grown quite attached to.
I could propagate them and have multiples of
any particular green gurl   I was impressed with
the whole idea. If there was any plant I wanted to
propagate first, it would be my very first plant, my
lush, viny Marble Queen pothos. She is a kween
I would want above all else to be preserved and
not have confined to just one planter. Dahling, this
kween dove into her propagation research to learn
all she could. Four years later, dahling, and I have
a bunch of her cuttings just thriving throughout
my apartment, and in the homes of my frands and
family. It's a lush and lovely situation.

Now, gurl, I know that propagating plants is not
always easy, and can sometimes bring up feelings
of anxiety. The last thang any plant parent wants
to see is a plant cutting that didn't make it! I have
had my fair share of plant parent propagating fails
throughout the years, but with some practice,
dedication to learning how to do better, and
patience, this kween has some techniques down
when it comes to particular green lil kweens.
Here are a couple of different plant propagation
techniques that I have learned about throughout
the years and have had a bit of fun with during this
lush journey.

STEM CUTTINGS

WHEN IT COMES TO my viny and multistemmed green gurls, a lil stem-cutting action is always my go-to when I want to grow lil baby kweens from the mature mother plant. I've done stem cuttings with a variety of pothos, heartleaf philodendrons, a collection of *Pileas*, and various begonias, but my favorite and most successful stem-cutting propagation moment is with the infamous Ms. *Rhaphidophora tetrasperma* herself!

STEP 1 Identify a mature stem on this kween that does not have any baby or budding leaves. I've found that cutting young leaves off from their root system usually results in those younger leaves not surviving during the propagation process.

STEP 2 Now that you have identified the mature stem, look for a tiny brown root node or aerial roots. This lil node or aerial roots will eventually support a whole root system for this cutting, to serve all that new growth realness. Cut diagonally 2 to 3

inches below the node with a sterilized pair of shears. QUICK NOTE: I use 70 to 100 percent isopropyl alcohol to sterilze my shears.

STEP 3 Remove any leaves that are close to the node so that those

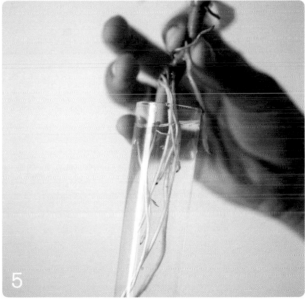

nodes can have room to breathe and grow into their lushness.

STEP 4 Place the cutting into a glass vessel filled with water and make sure that it is suspended in the water, not touching the bottom of the vessel. Place that kween in a sunny spot where she can soak up some bright, indirect light. Strong direct light or low-light conditions is not these cuttings' scene.

STEP 5 Patience, dahling! Let that cutting sit for a few weeks and check in on her every once in a while. If the water gets murky or she drinks it up, give her some fresh new tepid water. Sit back and enjoy watching her roots grow. Once her roots are 4 to 5 inches long, feel free to pot that kween into some fresh, well-drained, dampened soil.

LEAF CUTTINGS

OUR GREEN GURLS ARE DIVERSE lil creatures, so I've found it to be quite important to learn which propagation technique werks best with certain kweens, and leaf-cutting propagation has werked wonders for many of my succulent green gurls. Fun lil fact: Many types of succulent kweens grow tiny versions of the mother plant from their fallen or cut leaves. I have had particular success with this method in propagating one of my all-time favorite green gurls, Ms. *Sansevieria* (aka the snake plant).

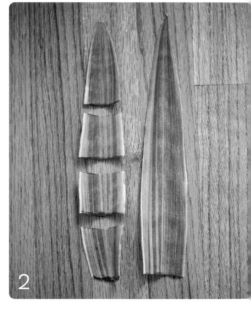

STEP 1 Identify a mature leaf that looks like she is ready to venture out on her own.

STEP 2 With a sterilized pair of shears, make a cut from the bottom of the leaf, detaching it from the mother plant. If your goal is to grow this leaf just as it is, let the cutting callous over for a day or two and then move on to step 3, dahling. If you want to make multiple cuttings from the one leaf, then continue to make multiple angled cuts to produce a few or several leaf cuttings. Remember which parts of the cuttings are the bottom ends. Let these cuttings callous over for a day or two.

STEP 3 Place the bottom end of the cutting into moist potting soil or suspend the cutting in water to watch her roots grow 2 to 3 inches

"Putting on my lil science hat and experimenting with my green gurls through various propagation methods has been a fun process for me as a plant parent."

3

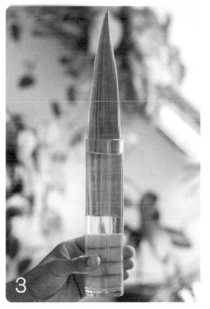

3

4

before placing her in moist potting soil. When I am doing multiple smaller cuttings of a single leaf, I tend to place them in soil; when I am propagating the whole leaf just as it is, I tend to place the cutting into water to let her roots grow a bit before placing her in soil. Both

methods have werked wonders for this kween.

STEP 4 Place the cutting, whether in soil or water, in a sunny spot with bright, indirect light. If the cutting is in water, change the water if it gets murky or she drinks it up, and

watch those roots grow. If small cuttings are placed in soil, check in with them by feeling to see if any have gone soft to the touch, as this is usually an indication that the cutting will not take root. But don't worry, dahling, you have multiple lil cuttings to rely on.

SOIL LAYERING

THE PREVIOUS TWO METHODS of propagation involve cutting a leaf or a stem from the mother plant, but what if we wanted to prep the part of the plant we hoped to propagate prior to removing it from the mother plant?! Well, dahling, that's where the method of layering comes in! Soil layering is the process of bringing a stem or vine of a plant to the soil, adding some soil to submerge the stem/vine, anchoring it in place, and letting the roots grow a bit before removing that stem/vine from the mother plant. I have used this method with many of my viny kweens that become a bit leggy including a variety of pothos kweens.

STEP 1 Identify the vine you are lewking to eventually propagate. Because you are going to give this vine some time to grow her roots and grow a lil stronger before separating her from the mother plant, choose a mature vine or a younger vine with new growth.

STEP 2 Look for the brown root nodes along the stem and prepare to place those nodes into the soil by circling the vine around the edges of the planter. Take some small U-shaped pins (found at any plant shop) and anchor the vine into place.

STEP 3 Take some fresh potting soil and place it over the pinned vine and carefully submerge it in soil, making sure that the leaves are upright and ready to bask in the sunshine. Water this green gurl so that the new soil can settle around those lil root nodes.

STEP 4 After 4 to 5 weeks, get your hands a lil dirty and dig up that vine you covered with soil. You'll find that she has new roots where those lil root nodes were and is ready to be placed in a new planter by cutting her stem and repotting her.

NOTE: Layering can be done in a couple of ways. When it comes to soil layering, if you want to avoid having to dig up the stem/vine from the mother's planter, place the vine/stem in another planter (preferably a nursery planter) while she is still attached to the mother plant. After 4 to 5 weeks you can simply cut the stem/vine from the mother plant, and there you have it, dahling, a whole new green gurl!

"Air" layering is another way to propagate that is easier with aroids, which grow those beautiful aerial roots. Simply take a handful of wet sphagnum moss and wrap it around the root node or aerial roots you are hoping to grow + strengthen. Wrap the moss and root in plastic film and keep them in place with plant tape or Scotch tape. Let that root sit for 3 to 4 weeks, and when you unwrap it, you'll find a more developed root system that is ready to be separated from the mother plant and potted in some fresh potting soil.

ROOT DIVISION

SOMETIMES OUR GREEN GURLS are serving such new growth realness that they produce fabulous offshoots or cute lil pups from their roots that can be divided, thus giving you a whole new green gurl to pot and grow. I have used this method with a variety of snake plants, philodendrons, ferns, peace lilies, and cast-iron plants, but my fav green gurl to propagate through division is Ms. *Zamioculcas zamiifolia* (aka the ZZ plant.)

STEP 1 I find it easier to do a lil root division when I first welcome a green gurl into my home and she is still in her nursery pot. Nine times outta ten there are multiple green gurls in that nursery pot. Remove the whole plant from her pot. Massage that old soil from the roots and look for the potato-like roots (rhizomes). Gently tug them apart from each other.

STEP 2 Immediately place each pup into a separate planter filled with that fresh potting soil. Soak the soil with some delicious H_2O so that she can have herself a lil drink, and so that the soil can settle around the roots and rhizome.

STEP 3 Place your new group of green gurls in bright indirect light so that they can soak up that sunshine without experiencing sunburn. If it is late spring or early summer, give these kweens some plant fertilizer after they've been in their new soil for about a week to get them a boost to encourage new growth.

3

OFFSETS AND LIL PLANTLETS

WHILE OUR GREEN GURLS CAN GROW pups from the roots, many house plants also produce cute lil offsets or plantlets from their stems, serving tiny lil daughter realness of the larger mother plant. Some of these lil kweens begin to develop roots while attached to their mother plant, while others wait until they come in contact with soil before letting those roots spread with a lushness. These lil daughter plantlets are the perfect lil green gurls to grow and expand your plant fam. A kween that is the epitome of offset propagation is Ms. *Chlorophytum comosum* (aka the spider plant).

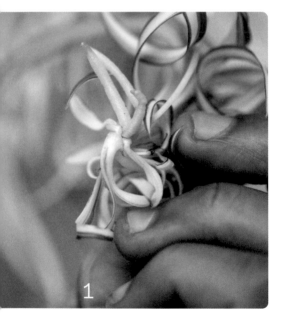

STEP 1 Take a look at the plantlets on your green gurl. Notice if any aerial roots have begun to grow from the lil kweens. Focus on the plantlets with established roots, as they are the ones that are a tad more ready to grow on their own. I often spritz the base of the plantlets with water every other morning to encourage those aerial roots to grow.

STEP 2 The day before detaching those semi-rooted plantlets, water the mother plant to ensure that she is lush and hydrated. Get a decent-size planter, fill it with fresh potting soil, and water the soil the day before as well. You'll use this for your plantlets tomorrow.

STEP 3 Take a few plantlets and with a sterilized pair of shears cut the stem that attaches them to the mother plant. Cut as close to the plantlet as possible so that you don't have a random stem sticking out from it.

STEP 4 Grab that planter with the dampened soil and arrange

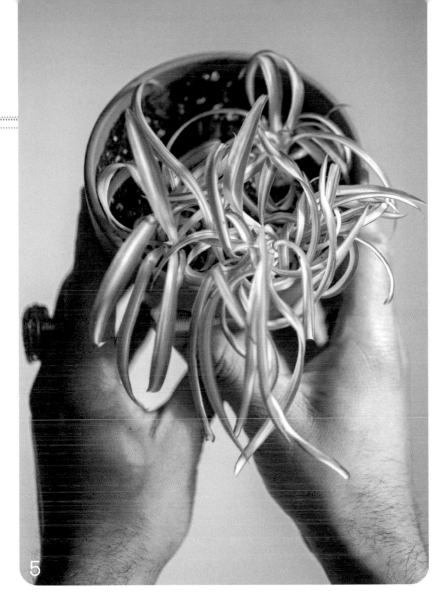

5

EVERY GREEN GURL'S ROOT growth rate varies, as do the other elements involved when it comes to propagating, dahling. Humidity, the average temperature in your space, the amount of sunlight that shines through your windows, and the health of the mother plant all come into play. My baby kweens usually start serving some new growth realness around week 2 or 3, but don't be discouraged if it takes a bit more time.

Putting on my lil science hat and experimenting with my green gurls through various propagation methods has been a fun process for me as a plant parent. I have also come to accept that with fierce successes, there will be some plant parent fails. Plant propagation can be tricky sometimes and a cutting or two may not make it through the process. But, gurl, that's why you either propagate multiple cuttings at the same time or simply try again. My biggest advice for kweens who are hoping to dive into this planty project is:

1   It is so crucial to do your research on the green gurl you want to propagate.

2   Patience is key when waiting for the green gurl to root (pot that cutting only when you feel her roots are strong and mature enough to take to soil).

3   And last, dahling, have fun with it, learn from your mistakes, and celebrate your successes.

the plantlets on the surface of the soil. Make sure each lil baby kween has space and room to grow in the pot. Keep the soil evenly and consistently moist by watering from the bottom on a schedule. Depending on the humidity, amount of sunlight, and temperature in your space that schedule may vary.

STEP 5 Once the lil baby kweens begin to grow longer and stronger roots, feel free to separate and repot them into their own planters; or if they are serving lush lewks as a group and they still have room to keep growing, then keep those kweens together.

CHAPTER 12

REPOTTING

Kween, are you ready to roll up those sleeves and get those hands a lil dirtay?! Welcome to the therapeutic earthy experience that is repotting.

THERE ARE TWO IMPORTANT THANGS when it comes to repotting your green gurls: new soil and, if needed, a slightly larger planter. The main focus when repotting your green gurls is providing fresh potting soil filled with the nutrients they love, enjoy, and need to serve new growth realness. After several months of watering your plants, nutrients in the soil are being either absorbed through the roots or flushed out through the drainage hole, depleting the soil of its nutritional richness. As a kween that regularly uses tap water to quench the thirst of her green gurls, I've also found that salts and various minerals can begin to build up in old potting soil. Tragic pests, bacteria, and mold can also accumulate in old soil, so it's best to occasionally give your green gurls' roots a nutritional change of scenery by providing her with fresh new potting soil.

kweens swimming in soil—the goal is to provide your green gurl with a lil extra room to grow into for the year ahead. I mark my calendars every year around early spring to begin my repotting adventures, right before growing season, as this is usually the best time to repot your green gurls.

Alright, dahling, now that we have gone through some of the basics, let's dive into identifying the signs that your green gurl may be ready to be repotted. There are three thangs you really want to be paying attention to: the overall health and growth of your green gurl, her roots, and the quality of the soil she's currently in.

LET'S TAKE A LOOK AT THAT GREEN GURL.

I'VE FOUND THAT sometimes I can simply look at my green gurl and tell that she needs to be repotted, without doing any further investigation. As you spend more time in your lil indoor jungle, you'll begin to get to know your green gurls, their growth patterns, and their little intricacies, and you'll begin to establish your own unique interactions with particular ones. I know many of my green gurls quite well and because of our history, coexisting in the same space, sometimes I can simply tell when they are ready for a change. It's a beautiful and fun rapport with the nature I have brought into my home.

If you can easily answer yes to the following questions, dahling, then your green gurl is probably ready for some repotting action:

→ Does your green gurl simply look too large for her current planter?
→ Does your green gurl tip over easily from the sheer weight of her fierce foliage?
→ Has your green gurl stopped growing or perhaps she's growing much slower than usual, outside of winter dormancy?

IN SOME REPOTTING SITUATIONS, I am not even changing the planter, but simply changing the soil. In other situations, it is clear that my green gurl needs more room to keep on serving lush lewks. I typically do a repotting assessment every 12 to 18 months with my green gurls, changing their soil at a bare minimum and assessing whether I need to give them a lil planter upgrade. I've repotted some of my kweens in their same planter for three-plus years, simply because they are slow growers and they still have room in their planters to keep on growing. For other green gurls I am upgrading the size of their planter every year because they have outgrown it. For these kweens I tend to go 2 inches larger than their old planter, but will go no higher than 4 inches larger if they have really pushed out that new growth since the last time I repotted them. I don't go any larger because while it may seem like a cute idea to go with an oversized planter to avoid having to repot a green gurl frequently, a planter that is too big for your green gurl could have some negative effects on her health. Larger planters mean more soil, which means more water, and if the planter is too big, that soil could take too long to dry out. Wet soil for long periods of time could lead to mold growth and/or the tragedy that is root rot, gurl. We ain't got time for none of that nonsense! We don't want our

IT'S ALL ABOUT THE ROOTS, DAHLING.

IF YOU HAVE NOT gotten to know the roots, the very foundation, of your green gurls, then, kween, I encourage you to get your hands dirty and check in on those roots occasionally, especially when trying to assess whether repotting is what your green gurl needs. While your green gurl is growing in all the lush ways about the soil, growth is also happening down below where space is finite. Those roots will continue to grow and expand over time, and eventually will have nowhere to go. They will begin to circle the pot, tightly wrapping themselves around each other, and will then begin to suffocate each other, negatively affecting the health of your green gurl. In this situation the roots are rootbound, and we don't want that for our green gurls, hunty. If you notice the following, dahling, then repotting that kween could be the best thang for her:

→ Those roots have begun to grow through the drainage hole of the planter cuz they are looking for more space.

→ Those roots are growing so lushly that they are raising that green gurl up out of her planter.

→ Those roots are becoming visible through the top layers of your green gurl's potting soil.

GET YO HANDS IN THAT SOIL, GURL.

SOMETIMES YOUR GREEN gurl does not need a new planter, she simply needs new potting soil with those rich nutrients. While you may be on a regular fertilizing schedule during those lush spring and summer months, and could be aerating that soil by poking holes into it with a chopstick, that may not be enough for your green gurl. That kween could be looking for a change of soil scenery, dahling. Here are some thangs you may notice about the soil that could indicate that your green gurl is ready for a new soil-mate:

→ That soil is drying out quicker than usual, and you find yourself giving your green gurl an extra drink or two of water to keep her happy.

→ When you water, the water stagnates and sits at the top of the soil, taking a lengthy amount of time to be absorbed

→ There is noticeable salt and mineral buildup on your green gurl's leaves and on her planter.

NOW THAT WE have chatted through some of the signs that your green gurl may need to be repotted, let's get into the actual process of this therapeutic activity! Here is what you need to get started:

1. **Fresh potting mix.** Make sure you've done your research on the best potting soil mixture that works for the green gurl you are repotting. Compost that old soil because you will not be reusing any of it.

2. **A trowel.** This mini shovel will help in dislodging that kween from her planter because you may find that your green gurl has gotten a lil snugged in her planter.

3. **Porous filter.** I don't use one all the time, but sometimes it's helpful to cover the drainage hole with a coffee filter or any other porous material to prevent that new soil from coming out.

4. **New planter.** If your green gurl needs more room for those roots to grow, then you'll want to get a new planter that is about 2 inches larger than her current planter.

5. **Watering can.** It's always a good idea to give your kween a fresh drink of water after repotting her so that the fresh new potting soil can settle around those roots.

6. **Repotting tarp.** Whether you are outside in your backyard or inside your home, a tarp may be helpful to contain that beautiful mess you'll make when repotting your kween.

REPOTTING YOUR GREEN GURL

STEP 1
REMOVE THAT GREEN GURL FROM HER CURRENT PLANTER.

ON YOUR REPOTTING tarp, turn that kween sideways, gently grasp her stems and/or leaves, and give a lil tug. She may be snugged in her planter, so feel free to use the trowel to loosen the soil along the edges or to tap the bottom of the planter until she slides out.

QUICK NOTE: In some situations, you may find your green gurl stuck in her current planter. In that case you may need to break the planter apart to remove her without detaching her from her roots. This is one of the reasons I enjoy terra-cotta pots! They are inexpensive and they break easily with a lil tap of a hammer.

STEP 2
MASSAGE THOSE ROOTS.

IT'S TIME to get rid of that old soil, dahling. Gently massage the soil clinging to the roots of your green gurl until a majority of the soil has fallen onto your plant tarp. If you find that the roots are wrapped tightly around each other (rootbound), untangle them. The thicker roots at the base of the foliage are vital organs for your green gurl, so be gentle as you unbind them. It is okay if a small stray root or two breaks off as you untangle; your green gurl will survive.

STEP 3
PREP THE PLANTER.

BRING THAT NEW planter over to your repotting tarp—it's time to get it ready for the arrival of your green gurl. If you are using a lil porous filter, place the material at the bottom of the pot to cover the drainage hole. If you are using a planter without a drainage hole, place a layer of lava rocks or something similar at the bottom of the planter. This will lift up those roots and prevent your green gurl from sitting in a pool of water, which could lead to root rot.

QUICK NOTE: If you are reusing the same planter because there is still room for your green gurl to keep on growing, wash the planter and give it a quick rinse with some tepid water. Rinse out any old soil, salt, or mineral buildup so it's looking cute for your green gurl and her new soil.

STEP 4
ADD THE SOIL AND THE GREEN GURL.

ADD A LAYER of that fresh new potting soil, and pack it down, creating a sturdy foundation for your green gurl to rest her roots on. Add a second layer of soil and create a hole in the center that you can place your green gurl's roots into. Bring that kween over and place that green gurl in the lil spot you have created for her in the planter. Add some more potting soil, covering her roots and securing her in her new planter. Do not pack the soil too tightly, as you want her roots to be able to breathe, dahling.

STEP 5
WATER THAT KWEEN, AND ENJOY YOUR WERK.

WATER THAT GREEN gurl from the top—as the water travels down it will settle the new soil around her roots. Place that green gurl back in her lil spot in your space and marvel at the lil planty project you just accomplished!

REPOTTING YOUR green gurls can be a messy process, but it can also be fun and therapeutic. I've had virtual and in-person repotting parties with my friends and loved ones, and, dahling, it was a cute moment! Other times I'm solo, blasting my music and just enjoying the quality time with my green gurls. I've found that in these moments of revitalizing the foundation of my green gurls, I often think about the ways I may need to revitalize, reassess, and feed some love into the very things that keep me sturdy in life—the things that keep me grounded and centered. Make the moment and experience what you want it to be, kween, and enjoy getting those hands in that soil!

CHAPTER 13

THE SCOOP ON FERTILIZER

Just as our bawdies need the occasional vitamins to give us a lil healthy boost, our green gurls need the same, dahling. In their natural habitat our green gurls are exposed to many natural elements (rotting wood, decaying plant/animal matter, animal droppings, etc.) that contain a mixture of nutritional minerals that our kweens extract from the soil to serve new growth realness and lush lewks. Houseplants are not exposed to some of these external nutrients as they would be in their native habitats, so we as plant parents need to provide those nutrients by occasionally adding a lil somethang somethang to their soil: FERTILIZER, hunty!

"When I first started out on this plant parent journey, I underestimated the importance of amending the soil of my green gurls with fertilizer."

OUR LIL KWEENS NEED a number of nutrients and minerals to photosynthesize and grow in all the lush ways, but we are gonna focus on the top six:

Carbon, from CO_2 in the air, forms the backbone of our green gurls' biomolecules, including proteins, starches, and cellulose.

Hydrogen, from the water we feed our gurls, is necessary for building the sugars that plants feed themselves.

Oxygen, from the water and the air around them, allows our kweens to breathe. It plays a critical role in photosynthesis and is both stored for energy and released as a byproduct.

Nitrogen is a major component of chlorophyll—the green pigments that aid plants in absorbing energy from light—and also helps plants make the proteins they need to produce new tissues.

Phosphorus is crucial in stimulating the growth of roots, buds, fruits, and flowers, aka new growth realness. It does this by helping transfer energy between the roots, leaves, and flowers, and is also important in cell division and tissue production.

Potassium is essential in improving the overall vigor and health of our green gurls. It helps regulate the opening and closing of the stomata—the plant's pores—which helps plants move water, nutrients, and carbohydrates from one area to another. It also gives our kweens a lil boost in fighting off insect pests and diseases.

Houseplants are able to soak up carbon, hydrogen, and oxygen from the air around them and the water we feed them. This leaves us with nitrogen, phosphorus, and potassium, which are primary nutrients in most houseplant fertilizers, along with secondary nutrients in smaller amounts (magnesium, calcium, sulfur, iron, and boron). When I first started out on this plant parent journey, I underestimated the importance of amending the soil of my green gurls with fertilizer. Over time this led to my green gurls experiencing stunted and slow growth, weak stems, pale leaves, and reduced flowering—all the tragic symptoms of houseplants being under-fertilized. So gurl, let's get into a couple of thangs about houseplant fertilizer so that you can provide your kweens with the nutrients they oh so deserve!

TYPE OF FERTILIZERS

THE FIRST THING I had to learn was that fertilizers fall into two general categories: organic, or "natural," and inorganic, or "synthetic." Organic means that the fertilizer has been minimally processed and the nutrients are bound up in their natural forms. In general, the nutrients in organic fertilizers are not water-soluble and are released to the plants slowly over a period of months. When inorganic fertilizer is manufactured, some nutrients are extracted and bound in specific ratios with other chemical fillers. In general, these fertilizers are water-soluble and can be taken up by the plant almost immediately. Refined to their pure state, the nutrients in inorganic fertilizers are chemically stripped of substances that control their availability and breakdown, which rarely occurs in nature.

Throughout this botanical adventure I have used both organic and inorganic fertilizers, and there are pros and cons to each:

ORGANIC/NATURAL

PROS

IMPROVES SOIL: As the organic material releases nutrients, it also improves the soil texture, allowing it to hold water and nutrients longer. Rich in organic matter, these fertilizers also stimulate beneficial soil microorganisms.

WERKS SLOWLY: In order for organic fertilizers to do their thang, the soil has to break them down first, which means there is a slow release of the nutrients. This makes it very difficult to over-fertilize (and harm) your green gurls. This slow release also means that there is little to no risk of toxic buildups of chemicals and salts, which our green gurls will greatly appreciate.

ECO-FRIENDLY: These fertilizers can be renewable, biodegradable, sustainable, and environmentally friendly when used properly.

SAVE THOSE COINS: While you can totally purchase packaged organic houseplant fertilizer, you can also make good use of some of your household waste to create your own:

→ Eggshells contain calcium, which can be great for our green gurls. Boil the empty shells and use the leftover water as a fertilizer tea; or grind up the boiled eggshells and add them to the soil.

→ Banana peels contain high levels of potassium and small amounts of nitrogen, phosphorus, and magnesium. Cut the peels into tiny pieces and mix them in with the soil, or puree them in water and pour into the soil. The peels will decompose and slowly release nutrients.

→ Used coffee grounds are high in nitrogen and relatively low in potassium and phosphorus. Mix coffee grounds into the soil and let the gradual nutritious magic happen.

→ Aquarium water is rich in natural nutrients from the decomposing fish food and fish waste. When changing your aquarium's water, simply pour some of the waste water into the soil of your green gurl.

→ Green tea is high in tannic acid, which is fabulous for our green gurls that love acidic soil (ferns, begonias, and African violets, to name a few). Twice-brewed and cooled green tea leaves can be mixed in with the soil.

CONS

IT'S A PROCESS: Organic fertilizer needs the help of microorganisms in the soil to be break down and then release nutrients into the soil—this takes time. This process can take months and your green gurl will not experience immediate results; patience is key. I've known some plant parents to add organic fertilizer to their green girls' soil in the winter so that it is broken down and released in time for the growing season.

NUTRIENT LEVELS: The nutrient levels/ratios in organic fertilizer are often unknown and the overall nutrient concentration is lower than that of synthetic fertilizer. This could lead to some inconsistencies in providing a sufficient amount of nutrients to your green gurls.

RESEARCH IS A MUST: When you purchase packaged organic fertilizer, do your research, as different products can provide different results. I've used some organic fertilizers that werked wonders and others that weren't so great. It helps to read and review any studies that have been done with the product.

INORGANIC/SYNTHETIC

PROS

WERKS QUICKLY: Synthetic fertilizers are water-soluble and can be taken up by our green gurls almost immediately. When synthetic fertilizers are manufactured, the nutrients are refined to their pure state and stripped of substances that control their availability and breakdown—this makes them readily accessible for our plant fam to absorb when we pour fertilizer into their soil. This can be quite helpful in quickly aiding any green gurls in distress from nutrient deficiencies.

N-P-K RATIO: Most of these fertilizers contain the three primary plant nutrients: nitrogen (N), phosphorus (P), and potassium (K). The N-P-K ratio is displayed on the package and allows you to match the needs of your green gurls to the ratio that best werks for them. For example, a ratio that reads 20-20-20 means that the fertilizer has 20% nitrogen, 20% phosphorus, and 20% potassium. The other 40 percent is actually just filler material or bulking agent. If you are hoping to get that foliage serving viridescent vibes, that may call for a higher nitrogen percentage. If you are trying to get one of your green gurls to flower, that may call for a higher phosphorus percentage. And if you are hoping to focus on pest and disease treatment or prevention, that may call for a higher potassium percentage.

CONVENIENT TO USE: Ready to use and with simple instructions to either pour directly into the soil or dilute with water, these fertilizers can save you some time when it comes to caring for your green gurls.

CONS

DOESN'T IMPROVE THE SOIL: While these fertilizers provide the fast-acting nutrients for our green gurls to soak up, they do very little when it comes to supporting the health and overall structure of their soil. These fertilizers do not contain organic matter, which is the main food source for those beneficial soil microorganisms. Packages often have labels that read "does not include the decaying matter necessary to improve soil structure."

LEACHING AND FREQUENT USE: If your green gurl's planter has a drainage hole and has that well-drained soil that most of our kweens enjoy, then it is inevitable that some of the nutrients will be washed out as we water the soil. This is called leaching, the loss of water-soluble plant nutrients from the soil. With fast-acting synthetic fertilizers, this means frequent application of these fertilizers is sometimes needed for our green gurls to experience a consistent boost of nutrients.

OVERFERTILIZATION BE REAL: Frequent use and the quick release of nutrients when it comes to these fertilizers also means that it can be easy to over-fertilize our green gurls. These fertilizers contain compounds and salts that plants are unable to absorb, and so remain in the soil. As the water evaporates it leaves the salts behind, you might find a white buildup on the surface of your plant's soil, around the surface of the planter, or around the planter's drainage hole. Over time these compounds build up in the soil, changing its chemistry, and can lead to root burn due to an overabundance of soluble salts. Here are some of the signs that your plant fam may be over-fertilized:

CRUST OF FERTILIZER ON THE SOIL SURFACE: This means that the soil structure is not ideal and that the minerals are not being absorbed by the plant, and are left sitting at the top of the soil.

BURNED ROOTS: If you are not under-watering or over-watering, and you check the roots to find that they are browned, blackened, brittle, or have turned to a mush-like state, then they may be experiencing root burn.

DISTRESSED FOLIAGE: Root burn eventually leads to yellowing, wilting, browning, or falling leaves. Those roots are damaged and cannot function properly, which means your green gurl is not absorbing water properly, leading to not-so-lush lewks. Plants that suffer from root burn often become stunted, wilted, and are often unable to flower.

NOTE: Over-fertilizing happens, dahling. Here are some thangs you can do that could help your green gurl get back to her lush lewks:

1 Remove any excess fertilizer from the surface of the soil. Do not remove too much soil, as we don't want to stress this kween out any further. One quarter of the soil is the max amount I usually remove.
2 Remove any wilted, yellowing, or burned leaves.
3 Leach the fertilizer from the soil with a nice long watering. Soak the soil and let water run out the drainage hole. As the water leaves the planter, it'll take that extra fertilizer, compounds, and salts with it.
4 Let that kween heal! Let the soil dry out and do not fertilize this kween for at least a month.

WHEN TO FERTILIZE

OUR GREEN GURLS are looking for that boost of nutrients during those active growing seasons, spring and summer. When winter rolls around, the decrease in that good ole sunshine, due to shorter days, and colder temperatures (depending on where you are in the world) send our kweens into a less active, dormant state. They don't need that boost of nutrients as often during these wintery moments. I simply decrease fertilizing to once a month during fall/winter.

If you are investing in packaged fertilizer, be sure to read the instructions, dahling. For many water-soluble fertilizers, weekly, biweekly, or monthly applications are recommended. Fertilizers do come in many forms—liquid or powder, time-release or organic—and should be applied appropriately for the utmost fabulous results. I've had conversations with some of my plants friends who fertilize with either slow-releasing or organic fertilizer in the winter, so that the soil microorganisms have time to break it all down and have those nutrients ready for their green gurls to absorb come spring. Like with all thangs, when it comes to this plant parent journey, intentionality and planning are key!

I tend to fertilize during my watering days, making note of the kind of fertilizer I use for a particular plant and how often the instructions say to apply. Like with most of my plant care routines, fertilizing is scheduled with care and intention. When it comes to fertilizing, I always try to remember that less is more, understanding that it is better to under-fertilize than over-fertilize. We just ain't got time for any root burn, kween!

CHOOSING A FERTILIZER

CHOOSING THE RIGHT fertilizer for your green gurls depends, dahling! It depends on the kind of green gurls you have, the conditions of the space you are growing them in, and your schedule. If you are a kween who is all about your green gurls serving lush foliage, then fertilizer high in nitrogen is the way to go. If you are a kween who has a bunch of flowering green gurls, then fertilizer high in phosphorus is the route to take. There are also specialty fertilizers for particular green gurls, so be sure to explore the options at your local plant shops and read those labels.

I'm a kween who loves to do my own little botanical experiments, so throughout this entire plant parent journey I have used different kinds of fertilizers: organic and inorganic (liquid, powder, and time-release). I have found that DIY organic fertilizers are fun and worth a try, but can be hard to manage and to supply for over 200 plants. Organic packaged fertilizers are great but are often a bit more expensive. I also have to plan out the application of this fertilizer in advance so that the microbes can break down the organic material and have the nutrients ready to be absorbed by my green gurls in time for growing season. Synthetic fertilizers can be easier to manage and can easily be fit into a weekly, biweekly, or monthly routine per the instructions. The tricky thing with these fertilizers is the risk of overfertilization, and, dahling, that has happened with some kweens in my plant fam more than once.

So, when it comes to fertilizing your plants, you have to pick your adventure, as all the options have their fair share of pros and cons. When making your choice, be sure to ask yourself: What kind of green gurls do I have? What nutrients do they enjoy most? How much time can I put into fertilizing my plant fam?

CHAPTER 14

THOSE #PLANTPARENT FAILS

Dahling, this plant parent journey would not be complete without the occasional plant parent fail—it's all just a part of the joys of gardening. I haven't kept count of the plants I've sent to the lil botanical garden in the sky, cuz she ain't about that life . . . but I have always used these unfortunate experiences as opportunities to learn, grow, and do better next time.

EACH TIME A PLANT LEAVES ME, I make note of what could have gone wrong. I inspect what's left of the leaves, I take a look at the roots, I note where the plant was placed in my apartment, and then I usually take the remains to my community compost bin. It's my way of ensuring that my green gurl returns back to the earth where she belongs.

Here are my top three plant parent fails and what I learned for the next time around, cuz if at first you don't succeed, give yourself grace and try, try, try again!

OVER-WATERING
AND UNDER-WATERING

FIGURING OUT HOW much is too much, too little, and just right when it comes to watering your green gurls can be tricky business. When I first began to build my plant fam, I was always concerned about them not having enough water. Gurl, a leaf would wilt, brown, or fall and this kween would grab her watering can. I thought the solution was more water, and this led to the tragedy that is over-watering. I then tried to reverse any damage I had done and prevent any further over-watering by skipping a watering or two. If I was giving them too much water, then obvi the solution was less water! Gurl, this only led to the calamity that is under-watering!

Five years into plant parenthood, I have a much better grasp on watering my plant fam, but it took time, patience, learning the symptoms my green gurls may experience when over-watered or under-watered, and creating solutions for myself to prevent this plant parent fail.

Sometimes the signs of over-watering and under-watering can look the same, so it's important to inspect your green gurl to figure out what exactly she is experiencing. Here are some of the signs your green lil kween could be going through water stress.

WILTING: A common thang for both over-watered and under-watered plants, so you have to check the soil to get a better sense of the situation. If the soil is wet, she's over-watered; her roots most likely can't breathe, are not functioning properly, and she's not pulling water from the soil. If the soil is dry, she's under-watered, thirsty, and needs a drink.

BROWNING EDGES: This happens with both over-watering and under-watering, so touch the browning parts of the leaves to get a better idea. If they are crispy and break off easily, under-watered. If they are soft and flexible, over-wattered.

YELLOWING LEAVES: Leaves turning yellow and eventually dropping off may be a sign that your green gurl is being over-watered. I've also seen lower leaves from some of my green gurls curl and yellow, which can be a sign of under-watering. I tend to check the soil to figure out which one it is.

MOLD OR FUNGAL GROWTH: Any mold, fungus, or small mushrooms growing on the top layer of the soil is a sign that the soil is staying moist for too long—this indicates over-watering.

SOIL PULLING AWAY FROM THE EDGE OF THE PLANTER: When the soil has shrunk away from the sides of the container, your green gurl is under-watered and would enjoy a nice soak.

DAMAGED ROOTS: It's all about the roots, dahling. If you are ever uncertain about whether your green gurl is experiencing water stress, check up on those roots. If the roots are mushy or slimy, then your kween is experiencing root rot as a result of over-watering. If the roots are crispy, brittle, and snap off easily, then your kween is under-watered and needs a drink of water ASAP.

OVER-WATERED, NOW WHAT?

If your green gurl is experiencing over-watering, don't fret! There is a chance that you can save her! First, prune any dead or dying leaves. These leaves can encourage pests and are using nutrients that your green gurl could use elsewhere. Second, take that kween out of her planter—it's time to give those roots a makeover. Remove any decaying or dead roots, and rinse the healthy remaining roots with some tepid water. Remove as much soil from the root ball as possible. Take that green gurl and place her in some fresh, well-drained dry soil. Let her heal and get adjusted to her new situation for 3 to 5 days before watering her again.

UNDER-WATERED, NOW WHAT?

Believe it or not, plants have a better chance of surviving under-watering than over-watering. So if your kween is under-watered, there is a good chance you can get that kween serving lush lewks once again! To revive her, she'll need a good soak. Place that kween in your tub or sink and let the water run through the planter and out through the drainage hole. It is important that the water touches all parts of the soil. If your planter does not have drainage, be sure to tip the planter over and let any excess water run out of the pot.

PREVENTATIVE SOLUTIONS

CHECK THAT SOIL: I routinely check the moisture of the soil of each of my green gurls by placing my finger 2 inches into the top layer (or, for larger pots, by using a soil probe, moisture meter, or simply by placing my finger into the drainage hole). If the soil is wet and clings to your finger, she doesn't need water right now. If the soil is dry and easily falls from your finger, then that kween could use a drink of that delicious water.

CHOOSE THE RIGHT PLANTER: When picking the planter that your green gurl will sink her roots into, give some thought as to which one may fit best into your plant parent routine. If you tend to over-water your plants, then you may want to invest in terra-cotta pots with drainage holes, as these pots are porous, which allows the soil to air out and any excess water to drain from the bottom of the pot. If you tend to under-water your plants, then you may want to look into plastic planters or ones without drainage, as these will hold on to that moisture longer. For any planters without drainage, place lava rocks at the bottom of the pot to ensure that your green gurl's roots are not sitting in any excess water.

ESTABLISH THAT WATERING ROUTINE: Having a watering routine has werked wonders in making sure that my green gurls experience minimal water stress. It allows me a designated time to check in on my plant fam and assess their watering needs. While I check in on some of my kweens (ferns and those green gurls that enjoy a steady, damp soil) daily, a weekly check-in is sufficient for most of the green gurls we welcome into our homes.

TOO MUCH SUNSHINE VS. NOT ENOUGH

WE'VE DIVED INTO the convo of water, now let's bask in the convo of that sunshine our green gurls love and adore. All of our green gurls need that golden sunshine in order to serve lewks, dahling, this we know. And whether she is labeled as a low-light, medium-light, or high-light kween, figuring out the right amount of sunlight for a particular plant takes time, trial, and error, and knowing the various signs of sun stress. In my previous apartment, making sure my plant fam had enough light was a constant struggle. With north-facing windows and various buildings blocking the minimal indirect light that came into my space, I had to get creative. I made a vow to myself and my green gurls that my next apartment would have south-facing windows, and that's exactly what she did. My current apartment has fabulous south-facing windows, and that direct sunlight peeking through is delightful—but it does come with its own challenges. Too much of a good thang is not necessarily ideal, cuz plants can experience sunburn. It's all about moderation and balance, dahling! Here are some of the thangs I have learned:

SIGNS OF INSUFFICIENT LIGHT

LEGGY GROWTH: With a lack of sufficient light your green gurl may begin to grow new leaves farther apart, causing the stem or vine to look sparse and leggy. This space between the leaves is called an internode. Lengthened internodal distance is a sign that your green gurl is lengthening her stems and vine in order to reach for sunlight. This can result in your kween serving not-so-lush lewks.

STUNTED GROWTH: Our green gurls need that sunshine in order to photosynthesize, feed themselves, and grow. You may notice that without sufficient light your green gurl is growing slower than usual or not growing at all. Lower light conditions can also lead to the growth of smaller than usual leaves.

LEANING: Our green gurls will do what they need to in order to catch that light, and sometimes they look like they're leaning toward the light source. Their leaves may also reorient themselves to face the light. If they are left in this situation, the side that faces away from the light source may look bare while the side facing the light is more full.

NOT ENOUGH LIGHT, NOW WHAT?

IF YOU FIND THAT YOUR kween is not getting enough light, the best thang to do is to switch thangs up and move her to a spot with more light. When I am increasing the sun exposure my green gurl gets, it is a gradual process. The last thang I want to do is shock my green gurl with full direct sun. Move that kween to a spot that has a bit more light, but not too much. Check in on that kween weekly to see if there is any new growth.

If she has leggy growth, trim back some of those vines or stems so that she can focus her energy on her foundational foliage. I like to propagate any leggy stems or vines! If she is leaning, be sure to rotate her occasionally, so that she is a well-rounded kween!

You can also get creative if you struggle with natural light in your space:

1   Invest in artificial full-spectrum grow lights.
2   Make your kweens mobile (on a utility cart with wheels) and follow the light.
3   If the temperature is right, move your kween outdoors to soak up some sunshine.

TOO MUCH SUN, NOW WHAT?

IF YOU FIND THAT you have given your green gurl too much of a good thang, then the best route is to decrease her sun exposure. Here are some thangs I have learned that have helped this kween bring some of her sunburned green gurls back to life and lewking lush:

1   If she is outside, take that green gurl back inside, and put her in a bright area. You want to slowly get her readjusted to bright, indirect light. If she is already inside, move her to a less sun-drenched spot.
2   She may be lewking dry, but lay off the watering, gurl. She needs time to breathe, and over-watering would not be a cute situation. Give her a nice soak a few days after she's had time to adjust to her new lil spot.
3   Trim off those burned and scorched leaves, hunty. They are not going to bounce back, so might as well give your green gurl a cute makeover.
4   Check those roots, hunty! They could have been damaged from the heat. If they are damaged, keep the soil moist but not soggy. The moisture of the soil can help repair the roots
5   Don't add any fertilizer, dahling . . . let that kween werk with what she has and give her space to heal.

SIGNS OF SUNBURN

DISCOLORED LEAVES: Too much sun can cause a breakdown of chlorophyll in our green gurls' leaves, and this could have her serving pale, bleached, and faded foliage.

BURNS: You may begin to notice blotchy specks of white, yellow, or brown on her foliage.

DRY TEXTURES: Too much sun can have your kween serving wrinkled, scaly, and crispy leaf realness, as the sunlight is drying up any moisture in her leaves.

THOSE TRAGIC PLANT PESTS

PLANT PARENTHOOD would not be the epic journey that it is without the battle that is fighting off those tragic plant pests. While I have been able to prevent and avoid major infestations (knock on all the wood), I do have the occasional visit from a pest or two that tries to get comfortable in my lil indoor jungle. Here are some of the pests my green gurls and I have encountered, and how I went about getting rid of them.

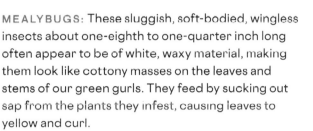

MEALYBUGS: These sluggish, soft-bodied, wingless insects about one-eighth to one-quarter inch long often appear to be of white, waxy material, making them look like cottony masses on the leaves and stems of our green gurls. They feed by sucking out sap from the plants they infest, causing leaves to yellow and curl.

HOW TO CONTROL

1 Isolate that green gurl from the rest of your plant fam.
2 Prune off any heavily infested leaves.
3 For other parts of the plant, take a cotton swab dipped in rubbing alcohol and wipe the mealybugs off of the leaves and stems. Insecticidal soap spray or neem oil can be used as well.
4 Do not over-water or over-fertilize, as these pesky kweens love high nitrogen levels and that soft new growth.
5 Check in on that kween regularly for the next 3 to 4 weeks, giving her the occasional spray of insecticidal soap or neem oil every 7 to 10 days.

THRIPS: These tiny, slender, and yellowish insects with narrow, fringed wings are about one-sixteenth of an inch in length and can be hard to spot on the leaves of our green gurls. They leap or fly away when disturbed, so beware, dahling! They feed by scraping surface cells to suck plant sap. Infested leaves may take on a silvery appearance or speckled discoloration.

HOW TO CONTROL:

1 Isolate that green gurl from the rest of your plant fam.
2 Prune off any heavily infested leaves.
3 Rinse off her foliage with some tepid tap water and let her air-dry.
4 Spray her foliage with an insecticidal soap or neem oil.
5 Check in on that kween regularly for the next 3 to 4 weeks, giving her the occasional spray of insecticidal soap or neem oil at night every 7 to 10 days.
6 Invest in some small sticky traps to catch any remaining adults that could be flying around your green gurl.

5 Keep the soil moist, not soggy, as spider mites thrive in drier situations.

6 Check regularly for the next 3 to 4 weeks, giving her the occasional spray of neem oil at night every 7 to 10 days.

7 Spider mites love dust, so dust off her leaves.

SPIDER MITES: These lil creatures are actually classified as arachnids and are more closely related to spiders, hence their name. Adults are reddish brown or pale in color, oval-shaped, and very small (one-fiftieth of an inch long). To see them clearly you need a magnifying glass, but the webs they spin are quite visible and are a distinctive sign that your kween is infested with these mites. Infested leaves begin to first show patterns of tiny spots on their leaves, which can lead to discoloration, curling, and, with time, falling off. Tight webs under leaves or along the stems are a sign that the spider mites are active and feeding on the plant sap of your green gurl.

HOW TO CONTROL:

1 Isolate that green gurl from the rest of your plants.

2 Prune off discolored leaves that are completely discolored and beyond saving.

3 Give her a rinse. For delicate plants, rinse lightly with tepid water and wipe the leaves and stems to remove any webbing. For sturdier plants, give a blast of water to remove any webbing.

4 Spray her foliage with an insecticidal soap.

FUNGUS GNATS: These creatures are some of the most common plant pests out there. If you're a plant parent, then nine times out of ten you've seen fungus gnats before—those small, delicate-bodied flies that live in the top 2 to 3 inches of your green gurl's soil. I remember noticing them when I watered my green gurls or disturbed the soil, causing them to take flight. Interestingly, adult fungus gnats do not bite or feed during their 7- to 10-day life-span. The larvae are the thangs we need to be wary of, as they feed on fungi, algae, decaying plant matter, leaves near the top of the soil, and the plant roots, which can cause yellowing, stunted growth, or worse.

HOW TO CONTROL:

1   Inspect the very top layer of your green gurl's soil and look for any whitish, glossy, clear larvae. Remove any infested soil from the planter.
2   Apply a fresh top layer of soil mixed with Mosquito Bits, as this insecticide will get rid of any remaining and future larvae.
3   These gnats thrive in humid and moist conditions, so be sure to let the soil of your green gurl dry out in between waterings.
4   Invest in some small sticky traps to catch any remaining adults that could be flying around your green gurl.

NOTE: You can also brew some concoctions, hunty! I have used a soap and water mixture (a cup of H_2O and a few drops of liquid soap), spraying it on the topsoil to kill larvae. I have also tried a hydrogen peroxide and water mixture (one part H_2O_2 and four parts water) to water my green gurl with, which kills larvae as well. I have also sprinkled ground cinnamon on the topsoil, which destroys the fungus that the larvae feed on. Using a combo of these methods has been quite helpful. I've also read about folks using vinegar, chamomile tea, diatomaceous earth, sticky traps, and sand on the topsoil (to prevent the laying of eggs) as other ways to manage gnats.

OVERALL PREVENTION, DAHLING

WHILE THE DIFFERENT techniques and strategies I have used to control any pest that pops up in my indoor jungle have been adventures worth exploring, I have found that prevention is the true key to dealing with this situation. It is oh so much easier to prevent these pesky creatures than to get rid of them. Here are some thangs to be mindful of as you werk to prevent these buggy botanical experiences:

→ Inspect any new green gurls before you welcome them into your home (whether new or just from outside) and isolate them for a few weeks before letting them meet the rest of the plant fam.

→ While these kweens are isolated, routinely check in with those green gurls, searching for any signs of pests. Check the undersides of the foliage, the stems, and the soil.

→ Wipe off your green gurls' foliage occasionally to prevent any dust buildup.

→ Give these green gurls everythang they need to serve new growth realness with a vigor, as stressed plants are more susceptible to pests.

→ Just a note: I occasionally engage in a number of the pest control methods I listed for each of the pests I have encountered, just as a way to further prevent or get rid of any pests I can visibly see. Yas, dahling, she's one of those plant parents.

CHAPTER 15

IT TAKES A VILLAGE

Building Community Through Plants

My plants, my green gurls, this beautiful botanical journey have provided me with a bridge to build community, connections, and friendships with some AH-MAZING folks, and I could not imagine this plantiful journey without them. Whether it's going on plant shopping adventures, trading lil lush clippings of our green gurls, giving each other plant parent advice, or sharing those plant parent struggles—it feels good to have a beautifully diverse community of fierce folks who are just as obsessed about plants as you are. Community care be self-care and self-care be community care, dahling.

> "There is a beautiful, diverse, and fierce community of folks out there who could talk green gurls for days!"

COMMUNITY BUILDING is not always an easy thang to do, but don't worry, kween—I got you! Here are some of the ways that I enjoy building community through plants:

LOCAL PLANT SHOP CHATS: Whenever I am exploring a plant shop, I enjoy connecting and chatting with the team that works there, cuz there's a 99.9 percent chance that they love plants as much as I do. It's also a great way to get to know the shop a lil better and find out a bit more about the green gurls they have sitting on their shelves.

BRUNCH + BOTANICAL GARDEN: One of my favorite routines is to treat myself to a lil brunch and a visit to my local botanical garden. Some days I'm taking a lil solo trip and I may bump into fellow plant parent regulars, or I'm bringing my frands with me to make a lil gathering out of this lush moment. Botanical gardens often offer events that folks can join, and are definitely worth checking out.

PLAN OR ATTEND A PLANT SWAP: I love trading plants, gurl—simply love it! It's the perfect way to bring your random plant frands together and share your green gurls with each other. Is there a green gurl that could use some pruning, leaving you with some healthy clippings? Is there a green gurl in your plant fam you know would probably do better In another plant parent's care? Well, gurl, see if any plant swaps are happening in your area or plan one yourself!

REPOTTING PARTIES: Repotting your green gurls can be a messy, fun, and therapeutic process, so why not make a party out of it, kween! Whether it's in person or virtual, I love gathering with my frands and creating new foundations for our green gurls to sink their roots into.

SIGN UP FOR A PLANT WERKSHOP: I'm a proud plant nerd and will take any opportunity to learn more about these lush green lil creatures. I've facilitated and participated in numerous planty werkshops, and I've always learned something new and made a new plant frand.

FACETIME PLANT PARENT SESH: Gurl, sometimes those plant parent struggles be having you going through it and sometimes you just need to vent! I've lost track of the number of times my plant frands and I call each other just to chat through some of our plant parent fails. It's fun to have a frand or two to bounce plant care ideas off of.

EXPLORE THE BOTANICAL SCENE: Whenever I visit a new town, city, state, or country the first thang this kween is about is exploring the botanical scene the place has to offer. What are the plant shops in the area? Are there any local botanical gardens nearby? Is there a national park that's worth visiting? It's a fun way to have a lil adventure with yourself and meet some new plant frands along the way.

START THAT GREEN GURL SOCIAL MEDIA ACCOUNT: The reach and accessibility of social media is so vast that it can serve as the perfect tool to connect with countless plant parents. I cannot put into words the beautiful experience it has been to connect with thousands of plant parents around the world through social media

EXPLORE THE LOCAL COMMUNITY GARDEN: Depending on where you live, there might be a local community garden that could be worth checking out and getting involved with! Community gardening projects always bring me joy and allow me the perfect opportunity to connect with my neighbors.

THE GREEN GIFTS THAT KEEP ON GIVING: Sometimes some of your frands don't even know they are plant people until you gift them a green gurl! Whenever I gift someone a green gurl, there's always a lil fun research involved, cuz she be that kind of plant parent, hunty:

1   What's their home sun lighting situation? Sticking with green gurls that can survive in a myriad of lighting conditions when gifting a green gurl to someone is always a cute way to go. Snake plants, pothos, ZZ plants are kweens that are great when it comes to tolerating lower light.
2   Are they a kween on the go or a homebody? Cacti and succulents are fab for those frands

that are on the go often, as they thrive with the occasional neglect. Ferns and orchids could be fun for kweens who are home more often and would enjoy a needier green gurl that loves a bit more attention.
3   Do they have any pets or small children? Our green gurls are wild lil creatures, so the occasional toxicity be all about survival but may not be suitable for certain homes, dahling. The parlor palm, the spider plant, or the prayer plant are three nontoxic green gurls that could be fab as a gift.

These are just a few of the questions I consider when looking to gift a green gurl to folks I love and cherish, and I find that a lil convo with the person I want to gift greenery to is always informative, fun, and simply lovely when gathering the deets that will be helpful in picking out the perfect plant for them. Match them with a green gurl and, voilà, you got another plant parent in your circle.

AS YOU BLOSSOM into your plant parenting journey, know that you don't have to do it alone. There is a beautiful, diverse, and fierce community of folks out there who could talk green gurls for days! As I have dived into the wonders of this lush botanical ride, I've always been open to meeting and connecting with the folks who my love of plants has brought into my life. And I feel blessed to have met each and every one of them. Plant frands be the best frands, gurl. The joy, the numerous botanical adventures, and the thangs I have learned from these beautiful folks are something I will forever cherish. I wish this for you, dahling! Dive into that lush botanical world, kween—a wild adventure awaits!

MS. BOSTON FERN

NATIVE TO TROPICAL REGIONS throughout the world, Ms. Boston Fern (aka Ms. *Nephrolepis exaltata*) is a green gurl serving full foliage realness. In her sultry natural habitat this kween decorates the scene with cascades of graceful, deep green fronds, and can grow as tall as a staggering 7 feet! I've always admired these plants and love how their foliage reminds me of my childhood afro—full, lush, and simply fierce, dahling!

I've found these kweens to enjoy that bright, indirect light, as too much full sun can burn that lush foliage. Utilizing sheer curtains for windows that get a lot of sun is the perfect situation for these kweens . . . filtered, dappled light is the mewd.

Like many of their fern sisters, these kweens enjoy light, loamy, and airy soil mixtures rich in organic matter. This soil texture allows the soil to stay moist, but also provides good drainage so the roots can breathe. Using a standard potting soil as the base,

I mix in perlite for air flow, compost for that rich organic matter, and peat moss for moisture retention.

She's a tropical kween, so warm, humid situations are her scene! I try to keep her soil consistently moist by utilizing plastic planters and checking her soil daily with a quick finger test. If she is not placed in a well-lit bathroom, I tend to have my humidifier by her side. She can be a tricky green gurl to care for, as she knows what she likes, but once you get that plant care recipe just right, she thrives with a lushness on the daily.

2 MS. STRING OF BANANAS

THIS —— IS BANANAS, B-A-N-A-N-A-S . . . literally! Let's shine that spotlight on Ms. String of Bananas herself, also known as Ms. *Senecio radicans*. Native to South Africa, this green gurl serves cascading vines of glossy, succulent, banana-shaped leaves, and can bloom tiny lavender, yellow, or white flowers that have a cinnamon-like scent during fall and winter. This succulent kween can be a fast-growing vine, reaching lengths up to a fierce 36 inches, and can be the perfect hardy green gurl for a hanging planter.

Like many succulents, this kween enjoys bright, direct light when grown indoors. I tend to keep my kween in a spot that gets four to six hours of direct sunlight throughout the day. I have also found that she responds well to artificial grow lights. When she does not get enough sun, her vines begin to grow leggy, less full, and new growth is more spaced out.

She is a succulent so I make sure not to over-water this kween, which could lead to root rot. Her soil is well drained and aerated, with fir bark, perlite, and sand added to the potting soil. With this soil mixture recipe, an occasional deep watering, and letting her dry out completely before watering again . . . she has been thriving! For this kween I've had to learn that it is better to under-water her than over-water her.

MS. SPIDER PLANT

LET'S WELCOME TO the botanical stage Ms. Spider Plant, aka Ms. *Chlorophytum comosum*! Gurl, these Latin names are literally fierce drag names and I am here for it! Native to tropical and southern Africa, these adaptable kweens have naturalized in other parts of the world, including the subtropical regions of Asia and Australia. Their grassy green-and-white leaves are always a vibe and I've come to enjoy seeing these kweens dangle in all their lush glory from their hanging planters. Surprisingly, this is a green gurl I've yet to welcome into my plant fam. To be honest, the kween is waiting for when she secures that chic loft apartment, so I can utilize those high ceilings and decorate by hanging a bunch of spider plants from above. She's all about delayed gratification and speaking thangs into the universe, hunty!

I've found that this kween can survive in a myriad of lighting conditions ranging from semi-shady to partial direct sun. I would probably stick with bright, indirect light for this kween, to avoid providing her with too little or too much sun.

Well-drained soil is the way to go for this kween. In the spring and summer months she does not like to be dried out for too long. Seems that keeping the soil slightly moist during these warmer months is the way to go. I've also read that this kween actually prefers a semi-potbound environment, so it is recommended to repot her only when she has visibly outgrown her planter.

These kweens are quite easy to propagate! Just make sure that those small spiderettes have developed roots before you pot them in some damp fresh soil, and you'll have a whole new green gurl for your space, dahling!

MS. PONYTAIL PALM

NATIVE TO THE STATES of Tamaulipas, Veracruz, and San Luis Potosí in eastern Mexico, Ms. Ponytail Palm (aka Ms. *Beaucarnea recurvata*) actually is not a palm tree at all. She is a member of the Asparagaceae family, which includes edible asparagus. Her foliage is fun, curly, and hardy, growing out of a bulbous woody stem. The earthy stem (caudex) of this plant is the source of her nickname "elephant's foot." In the wild these gorgeous trees can grow as tall as 30 feet. Gurl, there are even 350-year-old *Beaucarneas* registered in Mexico. She's a green gurl worth getting to know.

I've found this kween to thrive in bright light situations; bright, indirect light with a dapple of direct light every now and then is the best scene for this kween. In her natural habitat she is used to arid conditions. She stores water in her thick trunk so she can survive extended periods with no water, making her a great green gurl for plant kweens on the go! Before watering her well-drained and aerated soil, I make sure that it is completely dry. If dry, I give her a good soak, to ensure that the water has touched all parts of the soil and her roots.

And apparently she likes to take her time when it comes to new growth, but it's said that if given a bigger pot she'll grow at her own ease. She's a green gurl on her own schedule!

5 MS. CHINESE EVERGREEN

NATIVE TO THE TROPICAL and subtropical regions of Asia and New Guinea, Chinese evergreen (aka *Aglaonema*) kweens are a variety of green gurls that was first introduced to the West in 1885. Brought over to the Royal Kew Gardens those many years ago, this resilient and easy-to-care-for plant has been cultivated, hybridized, and bred into a wide array of cultivars. With more than twenty different varieties, this kween has foliage that can serve anythang from deep greens to a minty green, speckled to blotchy textures, and even variegated forms, gurl. In her humid, shady tropical forest habitat she often blooms cute little white flowers that resemble peace lilies.

These kweens are quite adaptable when it comes to lighting and can survive in low-light conditions. Like most "low-light" plants, I find that she thrives in bright, filtered indirect light. Too much direct light will certainly burn her leaves. Darker green varieties of these kweens enjoy more shade, while variegated varieties require a lil more light. I've also found that she does particularly well with artificial grow lights. She's a tropical kween so I keep her soil moist during the spring and summer, but I make sure the soil isn't soggy. Moderation is key, hunty! In the colder months when she is less active, she is watered thoroughly, but I make sure that the soil dries out between waterings. Adding peat moss (for moisture retention) and compost (for a dose of acidity) to the soil will have this green gurl growing for joy.

Overall, this green gurl is tough as nails, resilient, and has been one of the easier kweens to care for, which is why she was a part of my original plant fam when I first started this plantiful journey.

6 MS. MONSTERA DELICIOSA

NATIVE TO THE HUMID forests of Mexico, Costa Rica, Guatemala, Nicaragua, and Panama, this tropical kween is a fierce climbing vine. In her natural habitat, she can climb an impressive 70 feet into large trees, reaching up into the light that trickles through the canopy. Since she has both aerial roots and roots that dig into the soil, she's considered hemiepiphytic. The Latin name *deliciosa* refers to her "delicious" fruit that is edible only when ripe. Serving a combo of pineapple, coconut, and banana flavor realness, the fruit is ripe when the scales on the outside starts to come loose and the inside turns yellow like a banana. *Monstera* refers to how "monstrous" this kween can grow to be in her natural habitat. This kween is also known for foliage serving Swiss cheese realness. The technical term for plants making holes or clear parts in their leaves is "leaf fenestration," and is actually not unique to *Monsteras* (who knew!?). There are a ton of theories out there explaining why *Monsteras* grow holes in their leaves, but the leading one is that leaves with more holes tend to be bigger, with more surface area to grab sunlight that peaks through the dense forest canopy. I could go on and on about this kween, dahling . . . she's just THAT green gurl.

I've found these green gurls to be resilient and adaptable kweens. Bright, indirect sunlight is this kween's scene and she's all for those temps in the 65° to 70°F (18° to 21°C) range. She's a tropical kween, so she loves her some humidity! Invest in a humidifier, place it near this kween, and she be serving lush lewks. I water these kweens weekly in warmer months and every 2 to 3 weeks in colder months, letting that soil dry out in between waterings. These kweens can be fast growers, so well-drained + aerated soil has always worked well for my green gurls. This allows the roots to breathe, grow throughout the soil with ease, and ensures they are not sitting in moist soil for too long. A potting soil base with perlite and fir bark is my go-to soil mix recipe for these kweens.

7 MS. PRAYER PLANT

LET'S TAKE IT TO CHURCH with Ms. Prayer Plant, aka Ms. *Maranta leuconeura*! Native to the moist and swampy tropical forests of Central and South America, these kweens grow on the forest floor, never reaching more than 8 inches in height. These green gurls can be show-offs with their fierce foliage, oval leaves splashed with colors ranging from dark green patches to bright pink veins. These kweens also love to move! They open their leaves toward the sun in the morning to soak up that delicious sunshine and close their leaves as the sun sets. If you welcome this kween into your home or if you already have one, put a lil time-lapse on this kween and watch her dance in the sunshine.

In her natural habitat, this kween is used to growing in lower light conditions, catching the sunlight filtered through the canopy. I've found that bright, indirect light is her fav scene and that she is prone to sunburn with exposure to direct sun. Place her in that ambient bright, indirect light and let her leaves follow the sun. She enjoys her soil slightly acidic, so adding peat moss and compost to her well-drained soil is the perfect situation for this kween. In the warmer months I make sure to keep her soil consistently moist, and in colder months I have my humidifier blasting next to her.

8 MS. HOYA CARNOSA

MS. HOYA CARNOSA, also known as the porcelain flower or wax plant, is a green gurl I was excited to welcome into my plant fam. Native to eastern Asia and Australia, this kween has been in cultivation for almost two hundred years.

One day a kween was generous with herself and decided to welcome two *Hoya carnosas* into her plant fam. I had heard that *Hoyas* in general enjoy bright light, so I was a little hesitant because I knew that I had limited space and the lighting in my apartment was not the best. But the plant parent in me was determined, hunty!!!

Through my fun little experimentation I found that this kween enjoys bright, indirect light, that she does not do well in artificial light, and that her leaves burned when I put her in direct sunlight, so I placed her in an area that allows her to get at least six hours of bright, indirect light.

Like most green gurls, *Hoyas* are susceptible to root rot, so I've always made sure to let the soil dry out completely before watering. In the warmer months I water every week, and in the colder months, every 2 to 3 weeks

Once I found a spot in my apartment that Ms. *Hoya carnosa* seemed the happiest with, I made sure to keep her there. I did not have space for her twin sister so I gifted the second *Hoya* to a good frand who I knew had the space for her to thrive. My future goal for this green gurl is to repot her, as I've had her in the same pot for about a year now. I've read that *Hoyas* enjoy being rootbound, but I think it's time for a new pot cuz, gurl, she has grown. She is also an epiphyte so I will be getting a moss pole for this kween in the near future to allow her to climb.

9 MS. PENCIL CACTUS

AS THE ACADEMIC YEAR comes to a close, it only makes sense that I bring Ms. Pencil Cactus (aka Ms. *Euphorbia tirucalli*) to the botanical runway. While her nickname labels her as a cactus, she is actually a part of the Euphorbia family, hunty. Native to the semi-arid tropical regions of Africa and India, these succulent kweens can grow up to a fierce 30 feet in the wild, and about 6 feet indoors. Her branches are about the diameter of a pencil, hence her nickname, and when new branches sprout, they are often slightly pink and may have tiny lil leaves. Once she grows into her maturity, these tiny lil leaves will disappear.

I've always found this kween to be so easy to care for and she is a fun green gurl to jazz up any plant fam! When it comes to sunlight, she prefers bright, full sun, dahling! So put her on your brightest windowsill and let her soak up that sunshine. She is used to warm temperatures so make sure to keep her cozy with a 65° to 70°F (18° to 21°C) situation. She does not like cold drafts so pull her away from your window if it is not properly insulated. She is a succulent kween so she is good at storing water in her stems, thus enjoying drier soil. In the warmer months I water her every 2 to 3 weeks, and in the colder months I water her about every 4 weeks. When it comes to soil, she is all about that well-drained soil mixture recipe. I have mixed perlite, fir bark, and sand into her potting soil and she has been thriving, dahling.

10 MS. TOTEM POLE CACTUS

MS. TOTEM POLE CACTUS (aka Ms. *Lophocereus schottii*) is native to the desert regions of mainland Mexico and the Baja California peninsula of Mexico, and can grow to a fierce 10 to 12 feet in her natural habitat. This green gurl has been found growing in small populations in southern Arizona. I spotted this kween for the first time at an exhibit at the Brooklyn Botanic Garden and found it to be a cactus serving unique realness with its lumpy, bumpy, smooth exterior, a cactus without little spikes to prick your fingers . . . I had never seen a cactus like this before. Fun fact: This lack of spikes is a characteristic brought about by mutation. But when she grows to maturity, you're bound to see traces of her past spiky glory. About a month ago I was skipping through the Lower East Side and saw an intriguing set of cactus triplets amongst a sea of other cacti at a plant shop I was passing by. The shop had the cacti lined up along the sidewalk and as I glanced down, I spotted her immediately. Ms. Totem and I had reunited.

I've found that this kween enjoys a sunny spot with bright, indirect light. Yas, dahling, cacti can experience sunburn too if exposed to too much direct sunlight. Soaking this kween with water every 3 to 4 weeks in the colder months and every 2 weeks in the warmer months, and letting her well-drained soil dry out completely in between waterings has been werking wonders!

11 MS. EUPHORBIA LACTEA 'WHITE GHOST'

SOOOOOOOOOOOOO WE all have THAT green gurl that we are completely obsessed with and have multiples of them kweens, cuz plant parenthood be like that sometimes, hunty! Ms. *Euphorbia lactea* 'White Ghost' is THAT green gurl for me! I have seven of these kweens in my plant fam and, dahling, I don't plan on stopping there!

This kween grows wild in tropical Asia and is widely cultivated in the West Indies, Florida, and in many tropical areas around the world. Nicknamed the "false cactus," she is often mistaken to be a kind of cactus, but is instead a shrub and often grows in thickets in an upright columnar form to as much as 15 feet tall in her natural habitat.

I've found that this kween enjoys bright, indirect light with a couple of hours of direct light occasionally. Her white stems lack large amounts of chlorophyll, so too much direct sunlight can burn this kween. She does best if protected from strong sunshine during the hottest hours of the day.

While this tropical kween does grow in humid and wet climates, I water her like the succulent she is. In warmer months I water her every 10 or so days and every 3 weeks in the winter. I've used fir bark and perlite in her soil mixture to ensure proper drainage.

And, gurl, be sure to handle her carefully, as all Euphorbias ooze a milky latex sap when their stems break, which can be harmful to the skin and eyes.

12 MS. MONSTERA ADANSONII

NATIVE TO CENTRAL and South America, parts of southern Mexico, and the West Indies, this fabulous tropical vine is often found growing with a lushness in those sultry jungle and rainforest scenes. Much like her cousin Ms. *Monstera deliciosa*, she is known for the holes (or fenestrations) that develop on her leaves as she matures. Fun fact: The scientific term *fenestration* comes from the Latin word for "window." In her natural habitat her vines can stretch up to 20 feet, with her leaves reaching up to a massive 25 inches. This kween is a hemiepiphyte so she loves to climb, and in the wild can often be found sinking her aerial roots into trees and other surfaces, reaching for the sunlight shining through the canopy up above. In the spring months, she can blossom a beautiful cream-colored flower with hints of purple, but the conditions have to be just right for this kween and it is rare for her to flower when grown indoors.

I've found this fierce green gurl to enjoy bright, indirect light or filtered direct light, as too much direct sun tends to burn her leaves and we just ain't got time for sunburn. Well-drained soil is always my go-to for this kween, and I make sure to water her once a week in the warmer months and about every 2 weeks in the colder months. When I let her vines dangle from her pot, I've always found that her leaves are smaller and smaller, so to mimic her natural habitat I attach this kween to a moss pole so that she can grow upward in all her glory. I tend to mist her moss pole every morning as part of my lil routine to get my day started! She's used to those humid rainforest and jungles, dahling, so she loves a cute humidifier situation.

13 MS. DIEFFENBACHIA

SHE'S A TROPICAL kween native to Mexico and the West Indies south to Argentina . . . so, dahling, she is all about that warmth and humidity. These kweens come in a bunch of different viridescent varieties and hybrids, all serving fierce variations in size, leaf shape, and foliage coloring, hunty! This particular kween's full name is *Dieffenbachia bowmannii*, and I've found her to be an extremely resilient, fast-growing, and easy-to-care-for green gurl.

This kween does best in a filtered light kinda situation, where that bright sunshine shines through a cute sheer curtain. This kween has been producing adorable new tender leaves every few weeks that could be at a higher risk of sunburn if the light is too bright or shines directly on the foliage. So gotta protect the baby leaves, gurl. And because this kween is just a resilient and adaptable kinda green gurl, you'll also find that she can survive in lower light conditions as well.

She may be a tropical kween, but she doesn't like soggy soil, as this leads to that tragic root rot and we ain't about that life, dahling. I have this kween situated in well-drained soil (soil, perlite, and fir bark mixture) and water her once a week in warmer months, every 2 to 3 weeks in colder months. I always check to make sure the soil dries out in between waterings.

And just a lil note, gurl: she has a high toxicity level! This is simply a defense mechanism that prevents animals in the wild from messing with her. So keep this kween away from pets and kids.

14 MS. WATERMELON PEPEROMIA

GURL, WE ALL HAVE that plant or plants that are supposed to be "easy" to care for but as soon as we bring that kween into our homes she struggles, even though we've done our research . . . it happens, dahling. It's the territory that comes with being a plant parent! Ms. *Peperomia argyreia* (aka watermelon *Peperomia*) is a kween that I have struggled with in the past but is sometimes labeled an easy kween to care for.

These kweens are native to northern South America, including Bolivia, Brazil, Ecuador, and Venezuela, hunty. In their natural habitat these green gurls thrive in the undercover within forests with some sun and shade so it's best to try and replicate this. A bright room with indirect, ambient light seems to be werking well for my green gurl.

These kweens also enjoy humidity and their soil moist, but not soggy to the point that root rot becomes an issue. I've started using a peat-based soil mix, and my green gurl seems to be enjoying that.

Leaf propagation is also a fun lil planty project you can try with this kween. Start by choosing one of the healthier-lewking leaves, as dying leaves are less likely to root. Snap off the red stem and with a sterilized tool make a horizontal cut through the leaf. A lil 3- to 4-inch pot should do nicely; place some damp soil in the pot and make a lil slit in the soil. Place the leaves into the slits, about 2 centimeters into the soil, with the cut side down. Then, gently pack the soil around the leaves so that they're sturdily in place, hunty. Place in bright, indirect light and in a dome or plastic bag to keep the humidity high, which should werk well for this kween.

Keep the soil damp but don't water this kween until you see lil sproutlings coming out of the soil. It may take up to a month before you see any new growth, so be patient with her as she grows her roots.

15 MS. PITCHER PLANT

I REMEMBER WHEN I first laid eyes on Ms. Pitcher Plant (aka Ms. *Nepenthes* 'Miranda'). I was still a plant parent newbie and had never seen one in person before. She's a fan of *National Geographic*, so I knew a good deal about these plants, but never knew that folks actually grow them in their homes. A kween was simultaneously shook and intrigued.

This carnivorous green gurl is actually a complex human-made hybrid, her parents (*N. maxima* and *N. northiana*) are native to the tropical regions of Malaysia. There are about one hundred species in the *Nepenthes* family, and these kweens have the same number of chromosomes, making them very easy to crossbreed. . . gurl, look at science.

Nepenthes have two main divisions: kweens that grow in low tropical areas and kweens that grow high on the mountains. Both types require high humidity. Ms. Miranda, like the other lowland tropical pitcher plants, grows on and under trees. Dappled bright, indirect sunlight is what this kween enjoys. She also enjoys warmer temps and is sensitive to them low chills. I've found that peat moss works well as a potting medium, or a peat moss and soil mixture. I haven't fed mine any insects, but I've read that if you want to feed this green gurl, it's okay to drop in a few freeze-dried bloodworms, dead crickets, wasps, or similar insects.

ACKNOWLEDGMENTS

THE FIRST PERSON I have to acknowledge and thank for her magic is my mother, Katrina. Mom, you were more than a mother—my best friend, my home gurl, my fierce femme role model, my rock, my queen. Mama, you radiated an energy so passionate, so loving, so healing . . . folks gravitated toward your aura, basking in your greatness, love, and affection. You shared your gifts with this world so selflessly and effortlessly, it was just your phenomenal nature.

Rest in paradise, dahling . . . I hope it's as lush as your garden always was. We'll embrace each other again one day, we'll laugh at the memory of old times from years ago, it'll be like no time had passed at all. Until then, Mama, I'll tend to your garden and I'll make sure it grows so beautifully that you'll be able to see its colorful bloom from wherever you are in this universe. I love you, Mom, always and forever.

To my grandmother, the original plant queen, thank you for sharing your passion, joy, and love of gardening with me as a young child. You nurtured me and shined light on pathways and possibilities for me that I did not even know existed. I'm the author of my own joy and I have you to thank for showing me that I have that power.

To my loving father, Paul, and older brother, Marcus, thank you for all the unconditional love, support, and encouragement throughout this entire book-writing adventure! I would not have been able to write this book without your advice, guidance, laughs, and love. To my fabulous friends, Meredith, Ije, Deanna, Camille, and Claudia, thank you for the light you all bring into my life and for watering me when I couldn't water myself.

Thanks to everyone on the HarperCollins team, especially Lisa Sharkey, Maddie Pillari, and Lynne Yeamans.

Special shout to Phoebe Cheong for visually capturing each and every lush moment just the way I had envisioned it, and a HUGE thank-you to the New York Botanical Garden team and to all my fav Brooklyn plant shops—Horti, Crest Hardware & Urban Garden Center, Greenery Unlimited, Tula Plants and Design, The Sill, and Brooklyn Plantology— for letting us photograph in your lush spaces!

INDEX

ABOUT THE PHOTOGRAPHER

DAHLING, I'VE SAID IT before and I'm gonna say it again: plant frands be the best frands! This wonderful botanical project of a book would not be the viridescent lushness that it is without the vibrant green gurl imagery photographed by my dear friend Phoebe Cheong.

Photographer by day and plant parent 24/7, my BFF (best frond forever) has quite the collection of green gurls. Currently living in Brooklyn, New York, Phoebe has transformed her apartment into her very own lil exotic escape from the concrete jungle. Through her fabulous Instagram account, @ welcometothejunglehome, she documents her plant parent journey, adventuring into the joys of her ever-growing plant collection with the help of her adorable furry sidekick, Pixel the cat. As a brilliant visual storyteller, she embodies her lively energy through her work: a mix of color, natural touches, light play, and, of course, the lushness of her plant fam.

Phoebe and I met during the spring of 2019 during a plant parent panel discussion that was hosted by The Sill in Manhattan. For the rest of that summer, Phoebe and I continued to bump into each other. Whether it was a sale going on at a plant shop, an event at the local botanical garden, or a plant swap in the city, it was always such a fabulous time connecting with each other. Our passions for nature, our green gurls, our plant parent journeys were the bridge that led to a wonderful friendship. Plants brought my botanical bestie into my life, and for that I am forever grateful!

Working with Phoebe on the lush imagery for this book was such a joy! Her passion for greenery paired with her having lived and worked in major cities across Asia, Europe, and North America and been exposed to different cultures and environments inspires a creative energy that I deeply admire and wanted to have be a part of this book. Her creative eye and process helped me to see my own green gurls in a new light, from a fresh point of view. It was truly a fun adventure creating the moments and photos in this book.

Phoebe, you are one fierce photographer, plant parent, and friend, and I am so grateful to have werked with you on this! Cheers to the botanical adventures ahead, dahling, cheers!

ABOUT THE AUTHOR

CHRISTOPHER GRIFFIN (he/she/they pronouns) was born and raised in West Philadelphia, and is currently based in Brooklyn, New York, where they work in education and care for over 200 green gurls in their lil Brooklyn oasis of an apartment.

Being an educator at heart, Christopher started their Instagram account (@plantkween) in 2016 as a way to share the many lessons, lush adventures, and simple joys that come with being a plant parent. Their social media presence has been rooted in a journey of self-care, joy sharing, and community building all through the wonders of those green little creatures we call plants.

As a Black queer nonbinary femme, Christopher enjoys exploring creative and accessible ways to use plants as a vehicle to incite further conversations centering on Black joy and resilience, LGBTQ+ advocacy, and the need to increase the visibility, representation, and empowerment of QTPOC (Queer and Trans People of Color) in the lush world of horticulture.

Their aspirations are to continue to serve lush lewks and new growth realness right alongside their green gurls, have fun with it all, and bring folks along for the wild botanical ride.

Plant friends are the best friends!